FROM
VICTIM
TO
Victor

A Personal Healing Journey

FROM VICTIM TO VICTOR: A PERSONAL HEALING JOURNEY
Copyright © 2012 by Grace Gayle

Unless otherwise mentioned, all Scripture quotations are taken from the Holy Bible, New International Version®. Copyright © 1973, 1978, 1984 by International Bible Society. Used by permission of Zondervan Publishing House. Scripture quotations marked KJV are from The Holy Bible, King James Version. Copyright © 1977, 1984, Thomas Nelson Inc., Publishers.

ISBN:978-1-77069-513-9

Printed in Canada.

Word Alive Press
131 Cordite Road, Winnipeg, MB R3W 1S1
www.wordalivepress.ca

WORD ALIVE PRESS
Just Write!

MIX
Paper from
responsible sources
FSC   FSC® C016245
www.fsc.org

Library and Archives Canada Cataloguing in Publication

Gayle, Grace
    From victim to victor : a personal healing journey / Grace Gayle.
ISBN 978-1-77069-513-9

    1. Spiritual healing. 2. Suffering--Religious aspects--Christianity.
3. Gayle, Grace. I. Title.
BT732.5.M44 2012   234'.131   C2012-901305-6

To:

My loving, faithful husband, Paul,
My firstborn, Faith,
My daughter, Joy,
My son, Paul Jr., and
My two sons-in-law, Mike and Daryl.

In memory of Sylvia.

Lord,

Let the words of this book not be for my glory,
but for Your glory.
Let not the reader praise me for my ability to write
or my strength in walking through the healing journey,
but rather praise You;
for in Your grace, You have kept me.

Not to us, O Lord, not to us
but to your name be the glory,
because of your love and faithfulness.
(Psalms 115:1)

Let the words that flow from my mind onto the written page
be not my words, but Yours.
May the purpose of this book be to set other emotional prisoners free.

As wounded individuals find healing in Your loving arms,
may they learn to experience the feeling of Your love for them
in the deepest part of their emotions.

And I pray that [they], being rooted and established in [Your] love…
[may] grasp [understand] how wide and long and high and deep
is [Your] love [for them],
and to know [experience intimately] this love
[deep within their emotions].
(Ephesians 3:17–19)

I love the Lord…
for you, O Lord, have delivered
my soul from death,
my eyes from tears,
my feet from stumbling.
(Psalms 116:1, 8)

Amen.

TABLE OF CONTENTS

PART THREE: THE REDEMPTIVE JOURNEY

Preface

THE STONE QUARRY

In building the temple,
only blocks dressed at the quarry were used,
and no hammer, chisel or any other iron tool
was heard at the temple site while it was being built.
(1 Kings 6:7)

THE TIME IS THAT OF KING SOLOMON [IN THE BUILDING OF THE temple]. I caught sight of a plateau that seemed to contain an innumerable quantity of huge stones. Beyond the plateau was a vast hole where, obviously, stones had been cut...

Each stone was in a different stage of completion. Some were still shapeless masses of rock; others were huge rectangles, rough and jagged. Still others were glass smooth on one or two sides, while still coarse on the others. A few were complete, six sides almost glistening in smooth perfection.

After the stone is cut free from the earth, it is pulled here to the flat of the earth. The stone is then cut to an exact, predetermined size, chiseled with large, coarse cutting instruments until it has some semblance of shape, then cut with finer chisels... Next it is coarse sanded, then it is fine sanded, and last polished... [Each stone is cut, shaped and designed for a specific purpose.]

When the stone mason is finished, the stone is flawless. From here the stone is then taken to a distant city and to a building site. All these stones will be taken to that city. Each is destined to be taken to a place already determined... When this happens each stone fits perfectly into its place... They fit so perfectly, in fact, that they appear to be but one stone...

One day, when all these stones are completed, they will be taken to the site... There they will be taken through a Door, and from there to the building itself... where the stones are being reassembled. Reassembled, but this time into a house, almost as one vast stone...

At that site... on the other side of the Door, there will be no hammer, no chisel, no mason work at all. It is here, on this side of the building site, where all cutting, sanding and polishing must take place...

It is the plan of the Master Builder that all the business of making rough rock into perfectly fitting polished stone be accomplished in the stone quarry. There, there beyond that Door, is only the assembling together of what has been done here.

[Here on earth we live in the real quarry. We] are down [here]... being chiseled by God, people, and circumstances. But [we] are not alone. Every believer who has ever lived, those who lived before his visitation and all those who are yet to come... one day [we] will all be lifted out of this quarry through that Door...

Then shall no hammer [of pain or chisel of illness] be heard, for all of that is done in the quarry. Nor shall [we] be there as an endless array of stones. But together [we] will be assembled in one place, as one. A living city... the bride, The New Jerusalem.

There is but one place [we] will learn to follow him, to worship him, to obey him, to love him. Only one place, one time... to love him. Only one opportunity to be changed into his image. The place is [here]. The time… [our seventy years].[1]

---

1 Edwards, Gene. *The Inward Journey* (Wheaton, IL: Tyndale House Publishers, 1993), pp. 21–26.

Introduction

TEN-YEAR-OLD SHERRY BECAME DISCOURAGED WITH HER PROGRESS IN her physical therapy and wanted to quit. "Stop, Daddy, stop. It hurts too much. I don't want to do it anymore."

Her father, trying to be understanding and comforting, replied, "I know it hurts, honey, but you must do these exercises so that your legs can get strong again."

Four years earlier, Sherry had been in a train wreck in which her accompanying Aunt Betty was killed. Although Sherry had been badly injured—her legs having been crushed—she had survived. Her legs were now badly scarred and twisted, her recovery process slow and painful. After several surgeries and four years of physical therapy, Sherry still wasn't able to walk without braces on her legs and the support of her father's strong arms around her.

In her childishness, she blamed her father for having allowed her to go on vacation with her favourite aunt, which put her in the midst of the train when it tumbled down the mountainside. "Daddy, why did you let me go with Aunt Betty? If you hadn't, I wouldn't have been hurt."

One day, when her father insisted that she continue with her exercises, she sobbed, "It hurts too much every time I do those exercises. Daddy, why can't you love me just the way I am?"

Her father dropped to his knees, pulled her into his arms, pressed her head into his chest with one hand, and wiped away her tears with the other.

"Sweetheart," he replied, "I love you, I love you just the way you are, with all my heart. There is nothing, nothing that you could ever do to make me love you more. But I love you too much to let you stay this way. If I could take your pain for you, I would. I would give anything to trade places with you."

***

Sherry's story is much like my own, except it wasn't my legs that were badly scarred and mangled; it was my emotions. It wasn't a train wreck that devastated my life; it was the outcome of growing up in a dysfunctional family. I felt like crushed glass. I, too, cried out to my Father, but not my earthly father. I cried out to my Heavenly Father, "God, why didn't You protect me? If this pain is transforming me into Your likeness, stop. The cost is too great. God, if You love me, show me."

I asked my Heavenly Father to guide my healing process, give me the right books to read, and the right tapes to hear that would help me heal. God answered my prayers. He led me through a five-year healing journey which drew me into an intimate relationship with Him. He gave me a craving for studying His Word and spending time in His presence. Each time I cried out to my Heavenly Father in my agony, He answered me with a scripture or passage. By the end of the five-year period, God had given me over three hundred scriptures that helped in my healing progression.

Several times, I would ask Him a question only to walk into a Christian book store or church library in the next few days, march directly to a shelf of books, and find the answer in the first book I pulled out.

When asking Him why some particular situation was upsetting me, He would bring back to my memory scenarios from my childhood that paralleled my present experience. These parallel experiences would cause emotional pain from my past to flash forward to the present, making the present circumstances far more painful than called for. *"I will praise the Lord, who counsels me; even at night my heart instructs me"* (Psalms 16:7).

Our Heavenly Father loves us just the way we are, with all our brokenness, all our weaknesses, all our pain, and all our sin. But He loves us far too much to leave us hurting. His desire is always that we move beyond our emotional wounds and strive toward emotional and spiritual wholeness. We have a healer whose hands are reaching out, waiting for us to come to Him so that He can pick up the pieces of our lives and put them back together. Our Saviour has healing hands.

So my spirit grows faint within me;
my heart within me is dismayed.
I remember the days of long ago;
I meditate on all your works
and consider what your hands have done.
I spread out my hands to you;
my soul thirsts for you like a parched land.
(Psalms 143:4–6)

PART *One*

THE WILDERNESS JOURNEY

In a desert land he found [Grace],
in a barren and howling waste.
He shielded [Grace] and carried [her];
he guarded [her] as the apple of his eye,
like an eagle that stirs up its nest
and hovers over its young,
that spreads its wings to catch them
and carries them on its pinions.
(Deuteronomy 32:10–11)

 CHAPTER

One

OVER THE EDGE

Hope deferred makes the heart sick...
(Proverbs 13:12)

Our bones are dried up and our hope is gone...
(Ezekiel 37:11)

I FELT DEAD INSIDE

HEADS TURNED AND GLAZED EYES FOLLOWED ME AS MY HUSBAND and a nurse led me down the hospital corridor. No doubt they were wondering who this woman in her mid-thirties was and how she had ended up here. I had visited this hospital many times before and had given birth to my three children here as well. I had even visited someone in this ward once. Back then, I don't recall being stared at like I was now. But then, at that previous time, I was a visitor, visiting the mother of one of my Sunday School children, a person in a caregiving role; I wasn't a patient. I'm sure at this present time I looked just as dazed and confused as the rest of my peers, and the whole experience terrified me.

I felt dead inside; my soul was as dried up and barren as the Sahara Desert. I could almost hear God say, as He did to Ezekiel, *"Can these bones live?"* (Ezekiel 37:3) "Can breath still be breathed into this empty soul? Can her soul be restored?"

On my first night in the psychiatric ward, I was awakened to find several nurses in my room trying to force a patient in one of the other beds to take her meds. When she refused, two guards showed up and began forcing her from the room. Having been awakened from a deep medicated sleep, I was confused and asked what was going on. The nurse in charge harshly responded, "This doesn't concern you."

She was wrong; it did concern me. It concerned me a great deal. In fact, it concerned me so much that the rest of the night I lay terrified, trembling as I listened to the woman scream from several rooms down the hall. The next day, I saw her restrained in a bed a few doors down. I was petrified that they would tie me down, too, so I was very careful to do everything they told me.

One day when I was in the hospital, the psychiatrist came by while I was reading my Bible and asked me what I was doing. I said that I was reading my Bible.

"What good is that going to do you?" he asked.

"I believe it will heal me."

He laughed and said that he had never heard of such nonsense. He was wrong. Scripture says:

He sent forth his word and healed them; he rescued them from the grave. (Psalms 107:20)

For everything that was written in the past was written to teach us, so that through endurance and the encouragement of the Scriptures we might have hope. (Romans 15:4)

Each day, a nurse would come by to interview me, asking me all kinds of questions about my life and about the events that had transpired in the past year. "How long have you been feeling like this? What's been happening in your life? How is your marriage?" Every day brought a different nurse and every nurse had different advice. One would say, "You need to go back to work." Another said, "You need to go back to school and retrain." Still another, having noticed the conflict between my husband and myself, said, "You should leave your husband and start over." Every suggestion brought more confusion.

Then one day, an angel straight from heaven sat beside my bed and listened to me talk about my life and my failing marriage. She was older and more mature than the other nurses. She patted my hand and said, "Hang in there, dear. In a couple of years, you'll be glad you did." She was right. After a couple of years of counselling and healing, I was thankful that I had stayed in my marriage. It was the safest place for me.

Two good things came out of this experience. First, I was referred to a good counsellor by a friend of a friend. Second, although I left the psychiatric ward more confused than when I went in, God used all those questions the nurses had been asking to start me on my introspective journey, and from there the rebuilding of my life.

O God, you are my God,
earnestly I seek you;
my soul thirsts for you,
my body longs for you,
in a dry and weary land
where there is no water.
On my bed I remember you;
I think of you
through the watches of the night.
Because you are my help,
I sing in the shadow of your wings.
(Psalms 63:1, 6-7)

HE RESTORES MY SOUL

The Lord will surely comfort Grace,
and will look with compassion on all her ruins;
he will make her deserts like Eden,
her wastelands like the garden of the Lord.
Joy and gladness will be found in Grace,
thanksgiving and the sound of singing.

I will make rivers flow on barren heights,
and springs within the valleys.
I will turn her desert heart into pools of water,
and the parched ground of her soul into springs.

Her desert heart and the parched land of her soul will be glad;
her wilderness life will rejoice and blossom.
Like the crocus, it will burst into bloom;
it will rejoice greatly and shout for joy.
She will see the glory of the Lord, the splendour of her God.
Water will gush forth in her wilderness and streams in her desert.
The burning sand will become a pool,
the thirsty ground bubbling springs.[2]

2 Paraphrased from Psalms 23:3; Isaiah 51:3; Isaiah 41:18; and Isaiah 35:1–2,6–7.

 CHAPTER

Two

REFLECTIONS

Surely you desire truth in the inner parts;
you teach me wisdom in the inmost place.
(Psalms 51:6)

FACING THE DARKNESS

ALL THE QUESTIONS THAT THE NURSES WERE ASKING STARTED ME thinking about what had happened in my life in the past year. However, a person does not change from being a stable person to one out of control overnight. My problem went much deeper than the events that took place in the past year.

For as long as I could remember, I was troubled by two predominant emotions, one being fear and the other being loneliness. They were my constant companions. Though I managed at times to shake them for a short while, they would always return. There was no escaping them.

A story is told of a man who came to the realization that he was afraid of the dark. Later that day, as the sun began to set, the man ran after the sun to catch its light.

"Why are you running?" someone asked him.

He replied, "I'm afraid of the dark, so I'm running to catch the sun."

"If you chase after the sun, you'll forever be in the dark because you'll never catch it. You need to turn around, face the darkness, and walk toward it, and in time the sun will rise again."

The only way for me to heal was to turn around, face the pain, and work through all the painful memories with my Heavenly Father and a good counsellor.

> *Even though I walk through the valley*
> *of the shadow of death,*
> *[or through the darkest valley]*
> *I will fear no evil,*
> *for you are with me;*
> *your rod and your staff,*
> *they comfort me.*
> (Psalm 23:4)

Turn On Your Light

Lord, please turn on Your light,
illuminate all the dark corners of my heart.
Show me the wounded areas
that need a touch from Your healing hands.

Give me the courage I need
to face the truth about my childhood.
And Your Truth will set me free.

Give me strength, to let myself feel my emotions.
Such pain is necessary, that I may heal.

Healing takes time. Help me understand
that each painful moment today
may heal a memory of yesterday.

Cradle me in the palm of Your hand,
so that anything that enters my life
must be first permitted through
Your loving fingers.

Lord, I trust You, to guide my footsteps,
along Your chosen path, for my healing.
Amen.

THE EARLY YEARS

I was raised the youngest of seven children of a poor farmer. I had been added to an already large family where money was scarce and food was in short supply. Needless to say, the discovery of my conception didn't bring great joy but rather one of regret.

When I was six years old, I became the victim of a violent assault. I didn't understand what had happened to me; consequently, I was unable to tell anyone. I was severely traumatized, which presented in extremely high fevers and terrible nightmares, and I was subsequently admitted to a hospital several days later.

My mother carried me into the hospital room and left me with a nurse. No one had told me that I was being taken to a hospital because I was sick and needed to get well. I didn't know where I was, or why my mother had left me there. I was terrified and screamed for my mother. The nurse told me that if I didn't stop crying, my mother wouldn't be allowed to come back.

I stopped crying. I stopped feeling, and I buried the pain. However, the wound was still there; it just showed itself in different ways. Terror and fear plagued me, but I masked my emotions. Time and again, they showed themselves through high fevers and nightmares. Eventually, I was hospitalized once more.

My first year of school, being Grade One, turned out to be a pattern of not being able to learn because of fear, the teacher yelling at me for not paying attention, high fevers, nightmares, and absenteeism. Not surprisingly, I failed that year of school. That trauma resulted in me being labelled "a slow learner," and I developed very low self-esteem. It was several years before I was able to work at grade level, but eventually, with a lot of hard work, I made it onto the honour role in the eighth grade.

I was eight years old when my eldest sister left her husband and moved back in with us with her six children. This situation bumped me from being the youngest child to being treated as an oldest child. Somehow I managed to slip between the cracks of the two generations. I was too young to take part in activities with my older siblings, and although I was only twenty months older than my oldest nephew, I was considered too old to participate in the childish play of my nieces and nephews. This experience served to alienate me from my family, and although I lived in a large farmhouse with twelve other people, I was very much alone. Later in life, this experience kept me from feeling like I belonged as a member of my family or to any other group.

Alcoholism was an everyday occurrence in our home, resulting in emotional abuse and damage upon damage to my already wounded spirit. I had a very difficult time seeing myself as valuable. To benefit the growing family, I was often moved around from bedroom to bedroom like a piece of discarded furniture. This experience made me feel like I was always in the way, unwanted and worthless.

When I was a young child and adolescent, I craved the attention of adults, lapping up all I could get from them. I fantasized about being special to them and about being important to their lives. I was the type of needy, affection-starved child who is often easy prey for paedophiles. Such incidences robbed me of my self-worth. The long-lasting effects of such experiences crippled me in many of my adult relationships.

LIVING ON THE GOODER SIDE OF BAD

At age sixteen, I moved out of my parents' farmhouse to live in town. Not having a curfew and being too immature to set my own boundaries, I ran wild all hours of the night. I craved affection. This caused me to put myself in dangerous situations with boys who I didn't know very well. However, having witnessed the tragedy of teenage pregnancy, I was determined not to go there, and having seen firsthand the effects of alcohol abuse, I also avoided any involvement in alcohol and drugs, out of fear.

I had been taught to fear the wrath of God, through being told things like, "If you won't listen to me, God will deal with you, and you won't like His punishment." Looking back now, I realize that it was an attempt at keeping me from ruining my life. Nevertheless, such warnings caused severe spiritual damage in the way I viewed God. I began to see God as a cruel, disapproving God who demanded obedience in order for me to steer clear of His anger. I was afraid He would strike me with some terrible disease or accident. As a result, I tried to be good enough to avoid His punishment. I attended church regularly on Sundays and did "the lovely Christian girl thing," but on Friday and Saturday nights, I was out all hours, hanging out with people I shouldn't have been with. You might say I was living on the gooder side of bad—trying to be bad enough to have fun, but good enough not to get God mad at me.

I tried to play "the tough girl" for a brief period of time, but my pulling off the role was like someone coming along and auditioning my sweet little fifteen-pound Bichon Frise to play the part of a mean old junkyard dog. It just doesn't work.

At age nineteen, I had been dating a non-Christian young man for nearly two years and wanted to marry him, but it had been drilled into me that you never marry an unbeliever. So I began praying for God's blessing upon this relationship. One day as I was praying, I heard with the ears of my heart, "Give Me this relationship." I struggled with that decision for several days, and then I said, "Okay, Lord. He's Yours." Although he had been calling me long-distance three times a week, I never got another call from him after that night.

I went off to college that fall broken-hearted, depressed, desperately lonely, and entertaining suicidal thoughts. I spent the entire year running from my emotions, but still living on the gooder side of bad because I was afraid of God's judgement.

I had invited Jesus into my life when I was nine years old and God had put a "new song" in my heart (Psalms 40:3), but I had so much emotional damage that I couldn't live that new song. I buried it deep in a corner of my heart and often couldn't hear the melody at all. I was living the empty way of life passed down to me from my forefathers.

After college, I moved to Toronto. I became involved in the local church but still didn't have the power to live a victorious Christian life. Loneliness plagued me, eating away at me like a cancer. I often placed myself in situations that were dangerous, never being terribly bad, but not living a fruitful life, either.

MARRIED LIFE

Two years after moving to Toronto, I met my future husband. I wanted to find out if he was a keeper, so even though I was an inch taller than he was, I wore three-inch heels on our first date. His response was to go out and buy himself some platform shoes to bring himself closer to my level. I decided that he was worth getting to know. We were married a year later.

Not wanting to wait for a family, we had our first child eighteen months after our wedding. Three months after our first child was born, my husband had surgery on his right knee, followed by physical therapy, then more surgery and more therapy. He then had even more surgery, this time on his left knee, then again more therapy. I went back to work full-time to support our family when my daughter was six months old. By the time he was able to go back to work four years later, I had given birth to our second child.

We were nearly financially bankrupt and were forced to move our little family into a government housing community. We were told that the waiting list was up to two years, but the Lord pulled some strings and we were in within six weeks. We were given a ground floor apartment with our own entrance and fenced-in yard. This situation was perfect for running a daycare.

MINISTRY

When I saw the large number of children in the neighbourhood, I was determined to turn a bad experience into a fruitful one and started running Good News Clubs with Child Evangelism Fellowship, a widespread Christian organization responsible for creating great evangelistic programs for kids. After just six weeks, our club had outgrown the home we were in and we had to start a second one. God blessed our efforts, and by the end of the first year we had over eighty children in the two clubs. We closed the first year with an open house in the local school gym, which was attended by one hundred and fifty children and parents. The clubbers sang Christian choruses and presented the gospel through a puppet presentation of "The Lost Sheep." The following year, we added a Sunday School on Sunday afternoons in the building's party room.

An article was written up about our clubs in the local newspaper. Another group running activities for children stated off the record to the interviewer, "I don't know what they have going for them over there, but they ought to bottle it and sell it." Everything we tried to do took off. It was very evident that God had His hand on this ministry.

Seeing the overwhelming response to the clubs, my husband decided to attend Bible College. Since he had only been back to work for two years, after his four-year bout with leg surgeries, we didn't have money to buy suits to meet the dress code, so I prayed for a suit. We were answered by the providing of a heavy winter suit, which we praised the Lord for. However, September is often quite warm, so I again prayed for a lighter weight suit. The following Sunday, a lady showed up at church with three suits her son no longer wore, and two of them were lightweight. Again we were overwhelmed by the goodness of God.

While my husband attended Bible College, I ran a daycare in our home to provide for our needs. My memories of running a daycare remind me of what it feels like when someone makes a wrong assumption about you. The five children in my care ranged from my second child, being five years old, down to a one-year-old, each one being half a head taller than the next. They were every shade. My daughter was very fair with white-blond hair to one child being very dark. It didn't take a brilliant thinker to realize that they were all from different fathers.

As my routine was, I took them all to the laundry room with me and let them play there while I did my laundry. One day, a woman at the other end of the room said, "Get back there to your mother." I realized then that she thought all these kids were mine. To complete the picture, I was eight months pregnant with my third child at the time. By the way she looked at me with disgust, her expression pretty much said, "Bad girl!" I got a little glimpse of how the Samaritan woman at the well must have felt.

Although this was a very wrong assumption about me, sadly, for many women living in the community, this was their reality. I was very tempted to go over and introduce myself to this woman and tell her that I was the lady who ran the Sunday School in the building.

Before long I was leading a Sunday School, a Good News/craft club for kids on Tuesday evenings, and a ladies' Bible study one afternoon a week. Our home was also open to the teens and adults of the community to drop by whenever they needed to talk.

Sometimes we received a call during the night from a distressed parent or wife wanting us to visit or post bail for their son or husband who had been arrested. From time to time, we had to rescue children from situations of domestic violence until it was safe for them to return home.

Part of our ministry to the children who attended our programs was to visit them in their homes. One day when I was visiting one of the parents, I noticed a plant growing in the living room. I said, "What a lovely plant. What is it?"

The parent replied, "It's a marijuana plant."

I hadn't been taught protocol for an answer to that, so I said, "Well, it's a very nice one," as though I were an authority on the matter.

The drug dealers in the community opposed our ministry through continual threats to our lives. My husband was warned to watch out for his wife. The threat of rape frightened me half to death, far more than the death threats themselves. Our car tires were slashed, mud was thrown at our windows, our home was broken into and vandalized, and a Molotov cocktail was once thrown into the backyard of our townhouse, which we had moved into after our third child was born.

Therefore,
since through God's mercy
we have this ministry,
we do not lose heart.
For God, who said,
"Let light shine out of darkness,"
made his light shine in our hearts
to give us the light
of the knowledge of the glory of God

15

in the face of Christ.
But we have this treasure in jars of clay
to show that this all-surpassing power
is from God and not from us.
We are hard pressed on every side,
but not crushed;
perplexed, but not in despair;
persecuted, but not abandoned;
struck down, but not destroyed.
(2 Corinthians 4:1, 7-9)

 CHAPTER
Three

DETERIORATING HEALTH

You hear, O Lord, the desire of the afflicted;
you encourage them,
and you listen to their cry.
(Psalms 10:17)

SEVEN YEARS INTO THE MINISTRY, MY HEALTH BEGAN TO FAIL. IN THE preceding couple of years, I had been showing signs of burnout. I was exhausted, cranky, and frequently dropped into depression for several days at a time. We consistently asked for prayer for my health in our prayer letters, but my health continued to deteriorate.

My father then died of cancer, and several months later my closest brother also died of cancer. For some reason, I couldn't accept my brother's death. I would look for him at every family function. I didn't have the energy to deal with the grief of losing both my father and my brother in such a short span. I was unable to continue my daycare and had to give it up, along with the rest of our ministry.

Five months after my brother's death, I plunged into a deep depression, this one much too complicated for me to dig myself out of. The descent was like tumbling down a dozen flights of stairs, unable to catch hold of anything to stop the fall. I landed in the deepest, darkest pit you could ever imagine.

I had built a dam over the years to hold back my emotions so that I wouldn't have to feel them, but the years of threats and overwork had depleted my energy, and the final straw was the deaths of my father and brother. No longer having the strength to keep the wall erect, it came crashing down and the dam of emotion broke open.

Seemingly overnight, I went from being a person of very little emotion to one who was out of control. I no longer cried quietly, shedding a few tears, but was wracked with uncontrollable sobs. Where I would at one time have been a little ticked off, I now flew into fits of rage to the point that I feared I was going to seriously harm my husband or one of my children. Needless to say, all of this put a terrible strain on my marriage and caused extensive emotional pain for my children as well.

I spent too much time entertaining suicidal thoughts. It wasn't that I wanted to die, really; it was more that I couldn't bear living any longer with such overwhelming pain. Whenever I had to cross a street, a thought would fly into my mind daring me to step out in front of a truck.

I learned from Joyce Meyer's book *Battlefield of the Mind*[3] and Neil Anderson's books *The Bondage Breaker*[4] and *Victory over the Darkness*[5] that Satan uses our minds as a dumping ground for suicidal thoughts and other temptations.

I didn't know at the time that these were Satan's thoughts being dropped into my mind. Yet something held me back. It was like an invisible boundary was put around me, restraining me and preventing me from harming myself. I have no doubt that my friends and family were praying a hedge of protection around me constantly.

---

3 Meyer, Joyce. *Battlefield of the Mind* (New York, NY: Hachette Book Group, 1995). Faith Words Edition.

4 Anderson, Neil T. *The Bondage Breaker* (Eugene, OR: Harvest House, 1990).

5 Anderson, Neil T. *Victory over the Darknes* (Ventura, CA: Regal Books, 1990).

My husband had no idea I was so ill, until one day I expressed one of my suicidal thoughts out loud. This kind of thinking earned me an all-expense-paid holiday to a psychiatric ward for ten days. In the end, this experience put me in touch with a good counsellor who was able to help me get to the bottom of what was happening.

Why art thou cast down, O my soul? (Psalms 42:5, KJV)

Why so disturbed within me? Put your hope in God, for I will yet praise him, my Savior and my God. (Psalms 42:5–6)

Elizabeth George, in her book *The Lord Is My Shepherd*, gives a wonderful illustration of being cast-down.

> There's a beautiful picture for us here. You see, shepherds throughout time have applied the term "cast-down" to any sheep that's turned over on its back and can't get up again by itself. The scene goes something like this…
>
> A heavy, fat, or long-fleeced sheep will lie down comfortably in a little hollow in the ground. Next it rolls over on its side to stretch out and relax in the green grasses. But suddenly the center of gravity in its body shifts, pitching the sheep onto its back so that its feet no longer touch the ground! Despite the poor sheep's struggling efforts, it becomes impossible for it to turn upright.
>
> This is a sheep that is "cast down." And, interestingly, it's usually the largest and strongest sheep that are the most easily cast down! If it's cool or cloudy or rainy, a cast-down sheep can survive in this position for a day or two. But if the weather is hot and sunny, a cast-down sheep will be in critical condition in just a few hours! It's vital that the Shepherd arrive on the scene soon or the sheep will die.[6]

---

6 George, Elizabeth. *The Lord Is My Shepherd* (Eugene, OR: Harvest House Publishers, 2000), pp. 83–84.

On a warm day, the shepherd will count his sheep several times throughout the day to make sure they are all there. If one is missing, he will have to go back the way they have come and look for his lost sheep. Once the sheep is found, he then begins the process of getting the sheep back on its feet.

Restoring the cast-down sheep can be a tedious process, depending on the condition of the sheep and how long it has been cast down.

> If the poor sheep has been cast-down for some time, restoring it takes a great deal of patience, time, and care. First the sheep is gently rolled over. Then its legs are rubbed and massaged by the shepherd to revive circulation. Next comes the miserable sheep's head, which is propped up on the shepherd's knee and stroked and caressed and held for a time by its loving caregiver. Following this tender attention, the sheep is physically lifted up onto its feet by the shepherd. As the weak and wobbly sheep leans against the strong legs of its shepherd, the sheep takes its first few steps, fully supported by its master. It may take a full hour to get the sheep walking again, until finally it can stagger away on its own legs circling near the shepherd, who may have to rush over and pick his sheep up again… and again… and again. But the shepherd isn't done yet! For not until the sheep that's been cast down takes its first bites of green grass does the shepherd know that all is well. And so the good shepherd follows and checks up on his recuperating sheep… until it is fully restored.[7]

I was a cast-down sheep. I was down and couldn't get up. I needed someone to come alongside me and lift me back onto my feet. I needed someone to support me until I was strong enough to walk on my own.

Along with taking a bird's-eye view at where I came from, followed by extensive counselling while walking through all my painful memories, my healing process also required an in-depth study of who God is, and who I am as His child.

---

7 Ibid. p. 85.

I remember my affliction and my wandering,
the bitterness and the gall.
I well remember them, and my soul is downcast within me.
Yet this I call to mind and therefore I have hope:
Because of the Lord's great love we are not consumed,
for his compassions never fail.
They are new every morning; great is your faithfulness.
I say to myself, "The Lord is my portion;
therefore I will wait for him."
The Lord is good to those whose hope is in him,
to the one who seeks him;
it is good to wait quietly for the salvation of the Lord.
(Lamentations 3:19–26)

Strengthen the feeble hands, steady the knees that give way:
say to those with fearful hearts,
"Be strong, do not fear; your God will come…
he will come to save you."… Everlasting joy will crown their heads.
Gladness and joy will overtake them,
and sorrow and sighing will flee away.
(Isaiah 35:3–4, 10)

Though you have made me see troubles,
many and bitter, you will restore my life again;
from the depths of the earth you will again bring me up.
You will increase my honor and comfort me once again.
(Psalms 71:20–21)

I Am the Lord Who Heals You

What can I say for you? With what can I compare you?
To what can I liken you, that I may comfort you?
Your wound is as deep as the sea. Who can heal you?

"I will not completely destroy you.
I will discipline you, but only with justice;
I will not let you go entirely unpunished.
Why do you cry out over your wound, your pain that has no cure?
I will restore you to health and heal your wounds," declares the Lord.

I said, "O Lord, have mercy on me;
heal me, for I have sinned against you."
Heal me, O Lord, and I will be healed;
save me and I will be saved, for you are the one I praise."
O Lord my God, I called to you for help and you healed me.
You turned my wailing into dancing.
You removed my sackcloth and clothed me with joy,
that my heart may sing to you and not be silent.

It was I who healed them. I led them with cords of human kindness;
with ties of love; I lifted the yoke from their neck
and bent down to feed them.
I will heal their waywardness and love them freely.
I have seen his ways, but I will heal him;
I will guide him and restore comfort to him.

He heals the brokenhearted and binds up their wounds.
He wounds, but he also binds up. He injures, but his hands also heal.
He sent forth his word and healed them;
he rescued them from the grave.
Let them give thanks to the Lord for his unfailing love
and his wonderful deeds for men.

Praise the Lord, O my soul, and forget not all his benefits;
who forgives all your sins and heals all your diseases,
who redeems your life from the pit
and crowns you with love and compassion,
who satisfies your desires with good things
so that your youth is renewed like the eagle's.[8]

---

8 Paraphrased from Exodus 15:26; Lamentations 2:13; Jeremiah 30:11,15, 17; Psalms 41:4; Jeremiah 17:14; Psalms 30:1–2; Hosea 11:3–4; Isaiah: 57:18; Hosea 14:41; Psalms 147:3; Job 5:18; Psalms 107:20–21; and Psalms 103:2–5.

CHAPTER

Four

GOD, WHO ARE YOU?

O God, you are my God, earnestly I seek you;
my soul thirsts for you, my body longs for you,
in a dry and weary land where there is no water.
(Psalms 63:1)

BELIEVING THE LIE

IF YOU DON'T HAVE A HEALTHY VIEW OF WHO GOD IS, YOU CAN'T HAVE A
healthy perception of who you are as His child.

I believed the lie that the God of the Old Testament was an angry
dictator. Later, during my healing process, I discovered that although I
believed God loved me and sent His Son to die for my sin, I really didn't
believe at my emotional level that God loved me as an individual. I
never doubted my salvation, but I just couldn't grasp that He could love
me as a unique person. Contrary to what I had been taught in church,
my emotions told me that the God of the Old Testament was an angry

tyrant, while His Son, Jesus of the New Testament, was compassionate and caring.

I listened to a tape by David Seamonds, *Healing Your Concept of God,* in which he instructed his listeners to draw a picture of God. Not the God we have been taught about in church, but the one we feel in our emotions, in the way He thinks about us when we are on our knees. I drew a black blob.

As I thought about what I had drawn, I realized that I thought God was angry with me and enjoyed punishing me. It was like I was a pawn in a chess game, and God would put me in difficult situations just so He could take pleasure in watching me thrash around, trying to get myself out. In my emotions, I could hear Him laughing at me, enjoying my misery.

I needed healing in my belief of who God is. I began to cry out, "God, who *are* you?" I asked God to guide me into healing from the effects of being taught that He was angry with me.

I desperately wanted to have a God who loved me and cherished me for who I was, not for what I did. I needed a God who would love me even though my heart longed to have my own way and often rebelled. I needed a God who would not let me go, no matter how much I fought Him. I needed a God who would pursue me tirelessly until I came to the end of myself and was willing to hand over control of my life.

God answered my prayers by giving me a craving for His Word. I wasn't well enough to work, so I made "getting well" my full-time job. I spent three or four hours every day studying my Bible, making notes, and comparing other verses on the same topic. I copied out verses that spoke to my heart and read them out loud, several times throughout the day. I listened to tapes on inner healing and studied books written by pastors, counsellors, psychologists, and medical doctors on issues pertaining to my healing journey. I kept a journal and wrote about what I was learning.

JESUS IS WHAT GOD IS LIKE

I began studying about the life of Jesus through the first four books of the New Testament. Each time I read about an occasion where Jesus showed love and compassion, I would mark in the margins of my Bible, "Jesus is what God is like."

Then I read through the rest of the New Testament in search of supporting text and found several other verses that showed me what God is like. My purpose in doing this was to get it into my head, and consequently into the emotional level of my heart, that the God of the Old Testament and Jesus of the New Testament have the same character qualities.

Anyone who has seen me has seen the Father. (John 14:9)

[Jesus] is the image of the invisible God… For God was pleased to have all his fullness dwell in him. (Colossians 1:15, 19)

For in Christ all the fullness of the Deity lives in bodily form. (Colossians 2:9)

The Son is the radiance of God's glory and the exact representation of his being. (Hebrews 1:3)

The god of this age has blinded the minds of unbelievers, so that they cannot see the light of the gospel of the glory of Christ, who is the image of God… For God, who said, "Let light shine out of darkness," made his light shine in our hearts to give us the light of the knowledge of the glory of God in the face of Christ. (2 Corinthians 4:4, 6)

As I meditated on these words, the light slowly began to dawn on me that the God of the Old Testament had to have the same character qualities as the Jesus of the New Testament. While the truth of God's Word was making an impact on me intellectually, I still had a very difficult time reconciling these scriptures with those in the Old Testament where God punished His people with diseases, war, and exile.

How could I get from this place of knowing intellectually that God, by His very nature of holiness and righteousness, had to punish sin, to the place where I could feel His love for me in my emotions? I studied and meditated out loud on Scripture about God's love for me, and prayed for insight. I found the apostle Paul's prayer very helpful—

For this reason I kneel before the Father,
from whom his whole family in heaven and on earth derives its name.
I pray that out of his glorious riches he may strengthen you with power
through his Spirit in your inner being,
so that Christ may dwell in your hearts through faith.
And I pray that you, being rooted and established [securely] in love,
may have power, together with all the saints,
to grasp [understand, experience]
how wide and long and high and deep
is the love of Christ [for you],
and to know [intimately] this love that surpasses knowledge...
(Ephesians 3:14–19)

WHAT'S IN A NAME?

For to us a child is born, to us a Son is given…
And He will be called: Wonderful Counselor, Mighty God,
Everlasting Father, Prince of Peace.

Wonderful Counselor: [Marvelous Advisor]
I can tell Him about all my hurts, all my fears,
all my hopes, and all my dreams.
If I listen, He will guide me in making decisions;
He puts His desires into my heart.
For He knows the plans He has for me.

Mighty God: [All Powerful, All Knowing]
He is always in control, and nothing surprises Him.
I am His treasured possession;
He encloses me in the palm of His hand.
Nothing can touch me
without it first being sifted through His loving fingers.

Everlasting Father: [Never-ending Caregiver]
He is always available, always interested in what I am doing.
He is never too busy to listen to me, for He takes great delight in me.
When I am hurting, I can pour out my heart to Him,
and let Him encircle me with His arms of comfort.
He provides for all my needs—physically, emotionally, and spiritually.

Prince of Peace: [The Ultimate in Peacefulness]
In His presence I am totally content, for He is my peace,
and His grace is sufficient for me.
There are no worries, and no fears,
only a tranquility extended totally
and completely to His children.

For to us a child is born, to us a Son is given...
And He will be called:
Wonderful Counselor, Mighty God,
Everlasting Father, Prince of Peace.[9]

---

9 Paraphrased from Isaiah 9:6; Psalms 62:8; Psalms 37:4; Jeremiah 29:11; Deuteronomy 7:6; Isaiah 49:15–16; Zephaniah 3:17–18; Jeremiah 30:17; Isaiah 40:11; Ephesians 2:14; and 2 Corinthians 12:9.

CHAPTER

Five

GOD, IF YOU LOVE ME, SHOW ME

The Lord your God is with you, he is mighty to save.
He will take great delight in you,
he will quiet you with his love,
he will rejoice over you with singing.
The sorrows for the appointed feasts I will remove from you;
they are a burden and a reproach to you.
(Zephaniah 3:17–18)

I CRIED OUT, "GOD, IF YOU LOVE ME, SHOW ME!" GOD ANSWERED MY prayers by showing me scriptures in the Old Testament about His love for me as an individual, disputing my false belief that Jesus loves while God the Father is angry.

GOD'S LOVE IN THE PSALMS

I read about God's love through the Psalms, writing my own thoughts in the margins of my Bible as I interacted with what God was speaking to my heart. I dated each entry so that I would be able to look back and follow my progress.

You hear, O Lord, the desire of the afflicted; you encourage them, and you listen to their cry, defending the fatherless and the oppressed. (Psalms 10:17–18)

For he has not despised or disdained the suffering of the afflicted one; he has not hidden his face from [her] but has listened to [her] cry for help. (Psalms 22:24)

I will instruct you and teach you in the way you should go; I will counsel you and watch over you [as you walk your journey toward healing]. (Psalms 32:8)

The Lord's unfailing love surrounds the man who trusts in him. (Psalms 32:10)

The Lord is close to the brokenhearted and saves those who are crushed in spirit. A righteous man may have many troubles, but the Lord delivers him from them all. (Psalms 34:18–19)

God is our refuge and strength, an ever-present help in trouble. (Psalms 46:1)

No good thing does he withhold from those whose walk is blameless. (Psalms 84:11)

For great is your love toward me; you have delivered me from the depths of the grave... But you, O Lord, are a compassionate and gracious God, slow to anger, abounding in love and faithfulness. (Psalms 86:13, 15)

The Lord is gracious and compassionate, slow to anger and rich in love. The Lord is good to all; he has compassion on all he has made. (Psalms 145:8–9)

The Lord is faithful to all his promises and loving toward all he has made. The Lord upholds all those who fall and lifts up all who are bowed down. (Psalms 145:13–14)

He heals the brokenhearted and binds up their wounds. (Psalms 147:3)

In many of the Psalms, I was able to identify with the emotions of the writer. I noted in many cases that the psalmist started off the passage in emotional pain but closed it with words of praise. As I began to heal, my interaction with God followed the same pattern. I would begin by pouring out my anguish to God and end with praise.

It's as though I needed to empty myself of all my anguish by pouring out my heart to God before He could fill me with His peace. If a cup is already full of contaminated water, it needs to be poured out and washed before fresh, pure water can be put in and be of use to me, causing me to overflow with praise.

O Lord, how many are my foes [emotional scars]! How many [emotions and memories] rise up against me! Many [demons] are saying of me, 'God will not deliver [her].' But you are a shield around me, O Lord; you bestow glory on me and lift up my head. To the Lord I cry aloud, and he answers me... I lie down and sleep; I wake again, because the Lord sustains me... From the Lord comes deliverance... (Psalms 3:1–5, 8)

Answer me when I call to you, O my righteous God. Give me relief from my distress; be merciful to me and hear my prayer... I will lie down and sleep in peace, for you alone, O Lord, make me dwell in safety. (Psalms 4:1, 8)

Give ear to my words, O Lord, consider my sighing. Listen to my cry for help, my King and my God, for to you I pray. In the morning, O Lord, you hear my voice; in the morning I lay my requests before you and wait in expectation... For surely, O Lord, you bless the

righteous; you surround them with your favor as with a shield.
(Psalms 5:1–3, 12)

O Lord, do not rebuke me in your anger or discipline me in your wrath. Be merciful to me, Lord, for I am faint; O Lord, heal me, for my bones are in agony. My soul is in anguish. How long, O Lord, how long? Turn, O Lord, and deliver me; save me because of your unfailing love... I am worn out from groaning; all night long I flood my bed with weeping and drench my couch with tears... The Lord has heard my weeping. The Lord has heard my cry for mercy; the Lord accepts my prayer. (Psalms 6:1–4, 6, 8–9)

O Lord my God, I take refuge in you; save and deliver me from all [my emotional wounds] who pursue me, or they will tear me like a lion and rip me to pieces with no one to rescue me... I will give thanks to the Lord because of his righteousness and will sing praise to the name of the Lord Most High. (Psalms 7:1–2, 17)

THE LOVING HEART OF MY HEAVENLY FATHER

I read through Jeremiah and found the loving heart of my Heavenly Father. In the early chapters of Jeremiah, God pleads with His people to stop rebelling and come back to Him. He warns them over and over and over again of impending disaster if they do not repent and come back to the Lord their God.

In Jeremiah 7:30–31, I read about the depth to which God's people had fallen. Yet God continues to plead for His people to come back to Him. Finally, after years of pleading with His people and warning them of the coming punishment, God allows the Babylonian army to take them captive and destroy their land. They are taken into exile far from home. But God doesn't forget His people; in Jeremiah 29–33, God pours out His Fatherly heart for His children.

"For I know the plans I have for you," declares the Lord, "plans to prosper you and not to harm you, plans to give you hope and a

future... You will seek me and find me when you seek me with all your heart. I will be found by you," declares the Lord, "and will bring you back from captivity." (Jeremiah 29:11, 13–14)

"I will break the yoke off their necks and will tear off their bonds; no longer will foreigners enslave them. Instead, they will serve the Lord their God... I am with you and will save you," declares the Lord... "I will not completely destroy you. I will discipline you but only with justice; I will not let you go entirely unpunished... But I will restore you to health and heal your wounds," declares the Lord... "So you will be my people, and I will be your God." (Jeremiah 30:8–9, 11, 17, 22)

I have loved you with an everlasting love; I have drawn you with loving-kindness. I will build you up again and you will be rebuilt. (Jeremiah 31:3–4)

They will come with weeping; they will pray as I bring them back. I will lead them beside streams of water on a level path where they will not stumble... they will be like a well-watered garden, and they will sorrow no more... I will turn their mourning into gladness; I will give them comfort and joy instead of sorrow. (Jeremiah 31:9, 12–13)

Is not [this] my dear son, the child in whom I delight?... I still remember him. Therefore my heart yearns for him; I have great compassion for him. (Jeremiah 31:20)

I will put my law in their minds and write it on their hearts. I will be their God, and they will be my people... For I will forgive their wickedness and will remember their sins no more. (Jeremiah 31:33–34)

Wow! I was blown away! The thing that got me was that even after God's children had rebelled over and over and over again, God still loved them. His Fatherly heart grieved for them. In Jeremiah 29:11, God said that He still had a plan for their lives, even though they had really messed up. In Jeremiah 31:3–4, God said that He had never stopped loving His children, even though He had to discipline them for having rejected Him.

This wasn't the heart of a tyrant. This was the heart of a loving Father who wants desperately to have an intimate relationship with His children. If God feels this way about His rebellious children, then surely He must feel this way about me as well.

> *"For I know the plans I have for you, [Grace]," declares the Lord, "plans to prosper you and not to harm you, [Grace], plans to give you hope and a future… You will seek me and find me when you seek me with all your heart. I will be found by you,' declares the Lord, 'and will bring you back from captivity."* (Jeremiah 29:11, 13–14)

My Heavenly Father has a plan for my life even though I've run from Him. He has plans to favour me and make me successful. He gives me hope and a promising future. If I seek Him, He will bring me back from bondage.

> *I have loved you with an everlasting love; [Grace], I have drawn you with loving-kindness. I will build you up again [Grace], and you will be rebuilt.* (Jeremiah 31:3–4)

My Heavenly Father has never stopped loving me. He never wavers in His love for me, because His love doesn't depend on my performance. He never forces me, but draws me tenderly to Himself. He loves me because that is what He is. *"God is love"* (1 John 4:8).

Tears upon tears streamed down my face as the reality of God's love for me penetrated my heart. I was on the road to healing, but it was a long, slow process. Even though God had pressed His truth into my heart, my emotional wounds prevented them from taking root. Although I was a child of God, my emotional wounds had me living the empty way of life passed down to me from my forefathers for my entire life, and I wanted desperately to be free from it.

How great is the love
the Father has lavished on us,
that we should be called
children of God!
(1 John 3:1)

CHAPTER

Six

Expressions of God's Love

Let the beloved of the Lord
rest secure in Him.
For He shields him all day long,
and the one the Lord loves,
rests between His shoulders.
(Deuteronomy 33:12)

GOD'S LOVE IN ISAIAH

I READ THROUGH THE BOOK OF ISAIAH AND FOUND MANY WONDERFUL scriptures of God's love for me. I poured over this book like it was a personal love letter to me, spending hours at a time copying out verses and highlighting them in my Bible. Each verse was like a fresh cup of water to a sun-scorched desert wanderer, and I soaked them in like a sponge.

He tends his flock like a shepherd: He gathers the lambs in his arms
and carries them close to his heart; he gently leads those that have
young. (Isaiah 40:11)

"'I said, "You are my servant"; I have chosen you and have not rejected you. So do not fear, for I am with you; do not be dismayed, for I am your God. I will strengthen you and help you; I will uphold you with my righteous right hand... For I am the Lord, your God, who takes hold of your right hand and says to you, Do not fear; I will help you. Do not be afraid... for I myself will help you,' declares the Lord." (Isaiah 41:9–10, 13–14)

But now, this is what the Lord says—he who created you, [Grace], he who formed you, [Grace]: 'Fear not, for I have redeemed you; I have summoned you by name; you are mine. When you pass through the waters, I will be with you; and when you pass through the rivers, they will not sweep over you. When you walk through the fire, you will not be burned; the flames will not set you ablaze... Since you are precious and honored in my sight, and because I love you... Do not be afraid, for I am with you, [Grace]. (Isaiah 43:1–2, 4–5)

Listen to me, [Grace]...you whom I have upheld since you were conceived, and have carried since your birth. Even to your old age and gray hairs I am he, I am he who will sustain you. I have made you, [Grace,] and I will carry you; I will sustain you and I will rescue you. (Isaiah 46:3–4)

For the Lord comforts his people and will have compassion on his afflicted ones. (Isaiah 49:13)

Can a mother forget the baby at her breast and have no compassion on the child she has borne? Though she may forget, I will not forget you! See, I have engraved you on the palms of my hands. (Isaiah 49:15–16)

The Lord will surely comfort [Grace] and look with compassion on all her ruins; he will make her deserts like Eden, her wastelands like the garden of the Lord. Joy and gladness will be found in her, thanksgiving and the sound of singing... Gladness and joy will

*overtake them, and sorrow and sighing will flee away. I, even I, am
he who comforts you.* (Isaiah 51:3, 11–12)

*He has sent me to bind up the brokenhearted, to proclaim freedom for
the captives and release from darkness for the prisoners… to comfort
all who mourn, and provide for those who grieve… to bestow on
them a crown of beauty instead of ashes, the oil of gladness instead
of mourning, and a garment of praise instead of a spirit of despair.
They [the brokenhearted, the captives, the prisoners, the mourners
and grievers] will be called oaks of righteousness, a planting of the
Lord for the display of his splendour.* (Isaiah 61:1–3)

*As a mother comforts her child, so will I comfort you, [Grace]; and
you will be comforted…* (Isaiah 66:13)

GOD'S LOVE THROUGHOUT THE OLD TESTAMENT

I continually cried out to God for truth as I studied the rest of the
Old Testament in search of scriptures of God's love for me, and in the
process found many more wonderful verses. I kept gathering these little
gems as though my life depended on them, because it did.

*Let the beloved of the Lord [that's Grace] rest secure in him, for he
shields [Grace] all day long, and the one the Lord loves rests between
his shoulders.* (Deuteronomy 33:12)

*The Lord is with you when you are with him. If you seek him,
he will be found by you… But as for you, be strong and do not
give up [your healing journey], for your work will be rewarded.* (2
Chronicles 15:2, 7)

*For the eyes of the Lord range throughout the earth to strengthen
those whose hearts are fully committed to him.* (2 Chronicles
16:9)

But those who suffer he delivers in their suffering; he speaks to [Grace] in [her] affliction. He is wooing [Grace] from the jaws of distress to a spacious place free from restriction. (Job 36:15–16)

Trust in the Lord with all your heart and lean not on your own understanding; in all your ways acknowledge him, and he will make your paths straight [He will prepare the way for you]. (Proverbs 3:5–6)

…and He shall direct thy paths. (Proverbs 3:6, KJV)

I called on your name, O Lord, from the depths of the pit. You heard my plea; "Do not close your ears to my cry for relief." You came near when I called you, and you said, "Do not fear, [Grace]." O Lord, you took up my case; you redeemed my life. You have seen, O Lord, the wrong done to me. Uphold my cause! (Lamentations 3:55–59)

The Lord your God is with you, [Grace], he is mighty to save. He will take great delight in you, [Grace,] he will quiet you with his love, he will rejoice over you, [Grace,] with singing. The sorrows for the appointed feasts I will remove from you, [Grace]; they are a burden and a reproach to you, [Grace]. (Zephaniah 3:17–18)

I poured out my heart to my Heavenly Father as I read these verses out loud, over and over and over again.[10] I personalized each verse, putting my name in place of "you," "your," "he," "she," "him," "her," or "they." I interacted with them in my journal as I gave my response back to my Heavenly Father. Finally, I began memorizing them so that my mind could be renewed and His Word could take root and bear fruit in my emotions.

Do not conform any longer to the pattern of this world, but be transformed by the renewing of your mind. (Romans 12:2)

---

10 I recently learned that we believe more what we hear ourselves say out loud than what we read or hear anyone else say to us.

Eventually, I separated the verses into groups of common themes and arranged them into scripture collages.

I went for long walks everyday and read or quoted Scripture out loud as I walked, interacting with it in my own words back to my God. When I lay down to sleep at night, I would again meditate on the verses I had memorized, interacting with my Heavenly Father through them as I drifted off to sleep.

During the five years of healing, I discovered and wrote out more than three hundred verses and memorized at least half of them. In this way, the words and their meanings slowly began to change the way I felt about God as my Heavenly Father and the way I felt about myself as His child.

Within your temple [my heart], O God,
[I] meditate on your unfailing love.
(Psalms 48:9)

GOD'S LOVE IN EVERYDAY LIFE

My Heavenly Father continually showed His love for me through everyday events and through providing the right counsellor, whom I heard of through a friend of a friend. She, in turn, got me plugged into support groups, which I found very helpful in learning that I wasn't alone, that there are thousands of women just like me on the road to recovery.

As I healed, nature seemed to have deeper, richer colours than I had noticed before. I began to observe the varying blues of the sky, unusual cloud formations, and diverse shades of green in the foliage of the trees. I stopped by gardens and admired their many kinds of plants and colourful varieties. I paused, thanking my Heavenly Father for creation, for colour, and for eyesight, which enabled me to enjoy the beauty around me.

Another expression of God's love for me was how books and tapes ended up in my hands just when I needed them most. At one stage of my healing journey, when I was feeling desperately lonely, I prayed, "Dear Jesus, if You were to walk into this room right now, what would You do? Would You hold me in Your arms? Would You cry with me?"

A few weeks later, a friend handed me a book entitled *Hurt People Hurt People*.[11] I accidentally dropped it in my lap and it fell open to the most beautiful picture I had ever seen. The sight took my breath away. There in front of me was a picture of Jesus holding a weeping woman in His arms. I cried for three days straight. To know that my Heavenly Father loved me so much, that He would put this book into my hands so that I could see this picture and have a visual of Jesus holding me in His arms, shocked me speechless. A few days later, after the tears had stopped, I wrote this poem, and then cried some more.

---

11 Wilson, Sandra D. *Hurt People Hurt People* (Nashville, TN: Thomas Nelson Publishers, 1993).

Jesus, Did You?

Jesus, did You hold the wounded women in Your day?
Did You gather them in Your arms?
Did You draw them to Your breast?

Jesus, did You hold the woman of Samaria,
While she talked of all her years?
As she wracked with painful sobs,
Did You wipe away her tears?

Jesus, did You hold the adulterous woman,
When they threw her at Your feet?
Did You lift her with compassion?
Did Your hand caress her cheek?

Jesus, did You hold the weeping prostitutes,
When they cried out in their shame?
Did You squeeze their trembling shoulders?
Did You call each one by name?
Jesus, did You?

Jesus, would You hold the wounded women in my day?
Would You gather them in Your arms?
Would You draw them to Your breast?

Jesus, would You hold this wounded woman,
Shattered by rejection and abuse?
Would You rock her, oh so gently?
Would You heal her for Your use?
Jesus, would You, please?[12]

---

12 Paraphrased from John 4:4–29, 39–42; John 8:2–11; and Luke 7:36–50.

GOD'S PERFECT LOVE

I have loved you with an everlasting love.
I have drawn you with loving-kindness.
I will build you up again, and you will be rebuilt.
The Lord your God is with you. He is mighty to save.
He will take great delight in you. He will quiet you with His love.
He will rejoice over you with singing.
The sorrows for the appointed feasts, I will remove from you.
They are a burden and a reproach to you.

He reached down from on high and took hold of me.
He drew me out of deep waters.
He rescued me from my powerful enemy…
He brought me out into a spacious place.
He rescued me, because He delighted in me.

For you are a people, holy to the Lord your God.
The Lord your God has chosen you
out of all the peoples on the face of the earth
to be His people, His treasured possession.

There is no fear in love, but perfect love drives out fear,
because fear has to do with punishment.
But God demonstrates His own love for us in this:
While we were still sinners, Christ died for us.
Since you are precious and honored in my sight,
and because I love you… do not be afraid, for I am with you.

He tends His flock like a shepherd.
He gathers the lambs in His arms
and carries them close to His heart.
Let the beloved of the Lord rest secure in Him.
For He shields him all day long,

and the one the Lord loves, rests between His shoulders
...and nothing in all creation
will be able to separate us from the love of God
that is in Christ Jesus our Lord.[13]

---

13 Paraphrased from Jeremiah 31:3–4; Zephaniah 3:17–18; Psalms 18:16–19; Deuteronomy 7:6; 1 John 4:18; Romans 5:8; Isaiah 43:4–5; Isaiah 40:11; Deuteronomy 33:12; and Romans 8:39.

CHAPTER

Seven

GOD, WHY DIDN'T YOU PROTECT ME?

Why, O Lord, do you stand far off?
Why do you hide yourself in times of trouble?
(Psalms 10:1)

I PROTECTED YOU!

I HAD A LOT OF ANGER.

Someone once asked me if I was angry with God. I replied, "I can't be angry with God."

"Yes, you can," he said. "He already knows you're angry with Him, so you might as well be honest and talk to Him about it."

One day, early in my healing process, I stood in my kitchen screaming at God and asking, "Why didn't you protect me?" The Holy Spirit spoke to my heart and said, *I did protect you.* He showed me the time I had been assaulted when I was six years old. The situation could have been much worse. It could have been rape, but God had stopped it.

Then, over the next several days, God brought back to my memory numerous times through my teen years and early twenties when I had willingly placed myself in dangerous situations. The Holy Spirit walked with me through these memories and showed me how He had protected me.

The summer when I was fourteen, I got into a canoe and headed across a lake with six of my nieces and nephews. I was the oldest and the youngest was only five at the time. A friend of my sister had loaned the canoe to us. We had no life jackets and none of us could swim. I had never been in a canoe before and had no idea of the danger of the adventure. It would not have taken much to throw the canoe off balance, tipping it over to the death of all of us. Although there were adults on the shore watching, they would never have reached us in time. The hand of God was with us.

Later that summer, I was in a car with my sister and the same six nieces and nephews, plus the youngest one, speeding down the highway when she decided to pass a car. She misjudged the speed of the car she was passing and the oncoming traffic. Both the car we were passing and the one coming toward us had to hit the shoulder to avoid a head-on collision. This was before seatbelts were invented, not that they would have saved us. Once again, I saw God at work.

There was also the time when I was seventeen and I met a young man at a dance. I left with him and his friend at the end of the night to take a ride in his car. It was about 1:30 in the morning. We were driving down a country highway, slowing down at darkened laneways which I thought nothing of. A police officer pulled us over and asked to see each of their IDs and wrote down their information along with their license plate number. After that, they drove me straight home. It wasn't until the Lord brought that night back to my memory that I realized those two young men did not have good plans for me that night. God's protective hand had saved me.

When I was in college, I frequently hitchhiked with my roommate. One weekend, we went to her home one hundred miles from the college and on another we travelled to my home, sixty miles away. Some of the people who picked us up were rather creepy.

When I moved to Toronto by myself at nineteen, I lived downtown near Jarvis Street. I often wandered around by myself at night, talking to whoever talked to me. On more than one occasion I went for coffee with a total stranger. I was a little farm girl living in a big city with absolutely no street smarts. God reminded me that young people migrate to big cities every year and are befriended by pimps and then forced into prostitution.

God's hand of protection had overshadowed me my entire life. Given my poor self-worth and constant loneliness, I could have been easy prey for men who wanted to take advantage of me, but God made me strong in this area of my life so that I didn't become a victim of men who make empty promises. Each time I see an advertisement for United Way, and observe the hand above someone in a form of protection, I think of how God protected me.

Have mercy on me, O God, have mercy on me, for in you my soul takes refuge. I will take refuge in the shadow of your wings until the disaster has passed. (Psalms 57:1)

The Lord is my rock, my fortress and my deliverer; my God is my rock, in whom I take refuge. He is my shield and the horn of my salvation, my stronghold. (Psalms 18:2)

My eyes are ever on the Lord, for only he will release my feet from the snare. (Psalms 25:15)

He who dwells in the shelter of the Most High will rest in the shadow of the Almighty. I will say of the Lord, 'He is my refuge and my fortress, my God, in whom I trust.' Surely he will save you from the fowler's snare and from the deadly pestilence. He will cover you with his feathers, and under his wings you will find refuge; his faithfulness will be your shield and rampart. (Psalms 91:1–4)

Our Creator gave us a manual by which to get the best benefit from our lives. If we choose to ignore his guidelines, we will cause ourselves pain.

He is the Rock, his works are perfect, and all his ways are just. A faithful God who does no wrong, upright and just is he... Is he not your Father, your Creator, who made you and formed you? (Deuteronomy 32:4, 6)

Let's say I invent a new vacuum cleaner. As the manufacturer, I will write up a manual containing rules and regulations to get the best results from my invention and ensure the long life of the product. I will name the parts. I will say how it should be used and how it should be maintained. I will give directions on troubleshooting—if this happens, do this; if that happens, do that. Now, if you buy my vacuum cleaner and neglect to read the manual, you run the risk of ruining the machine or preventing it from working at its full potential.

Everything in creation has rules or boundaries for its protection. If we lie in the sun too long without sunscreen, we get burnt and feel pain. If we go out on a very cold day without gloves, our hands get cold or freeze and cause us a lot of pain. If we go out in the rain without rain gear, we get wet. If we jump from a tall building, the law of gravity guarantees we will not do it again.

Our Heavenly Father gave us His Word to guide and protect us from unnecessary pain. However, if we insist on venturing out from under God's protective umbrella, we're going to get wet. Sometimes I brought pain on myself and had to reap the consequences of my own foolishness and sin. At times, the only way to learn from our mistakes is to face the outcome of our behaviour. Even then, we don't walk through the consequences alone; God is always with us.

If the Lord delights in a man's way,
he makes his steps firm; though he stumble,
he will not fall, for the Lord upholds him with his hand.
(Psalms 37:23–24)

"Because [Grace] loves me," says the Lord,
"I will rescue [her]; I will protect [her],
for [Grace] acknowledges my name.
[Grace] will call upon me, and I will answer [her];
I will be with [Grace] in trouble,
I will deliver [her] and honor [her].
(Psalms 91:14–15)

For you have delivered me from death
and my feet from stumbling,
that I may walk before God in the light of life.
(Psalms 56:13)

You are my hiding place;
you will protect me from trouble
and surround me with songs of deliverance.
(Psalms 32:7)

REFLECTIONS ON PSALMS 139

"O Lord, you have searched me and you know me" (Psalms 139:1).

Lord, you know every tiny corner of the closet of my heart. You know every emotion I've ever felt.

"You know when I sit and when I rise; you perceive my thoughts from afar. You discern my going out and my lying down; you are familiar with all my ways. Before a word is on my tongue you know it completely, O Lord" (Psalms 139:2–4).

You know all my habits, Lord, both the good and the bad. You know my thought patterns, those that are healthy and honouring to You and those that are unhealthy which cause me pain.

"You hem me in—behind and before; you have laid your hand upon me" (Psalms 139:5).

You surround me with Your protection, Father, and give me a safe place to pour out my heart.

"Such knowledge is too wonderful for me, too lofty for me to attain" (Psalms 139:6).

I am overwhelmed at Your goodness to me. How is it that my heart keeps wandering away and yet You continue to forgive me?

"Where can I go from your Spirit? Where can I flee from your presence?" (Psalms 139:7)

Father, even when I turn and run away from You, You move in front of me and I have no place to run but into Your outstretched arms.

"If I make my bed in the depths, you are there" (Psalms 139:8).

Even in the depths of my despair, You have shown me that You are deeper still.

"If I settle on the far side of the sea, even there your hand will guide me, your right hand will hold me fast" (Psalms 139:9–10).

Even when I run away from my emotional pain, Your hand guides me toward healing and wholeness.

"If I say, 'Surely the darkness will hide me, and the light become night around me,' even the darkness will not be dark to you; the night will shine like the day, for darkness is as light to you" (Psalms 139:11–12).

Even when I choose to listen to Satan's lies and believe that You are tired of my crying out to You and that You really don't care, You speak truth to my heart. You remind me that You will never leave me or forsake me. You remind me that You have promised to walk with me through the valley of the shadow of every possible fear, hurt, and struggle.

"For you created my inmost being; you knit me together in my mother's womb. I praise you because I am fearfully and wonderfully made; your works are wonderful, I know that full well. My frame was not hidden from you when I was made in the secret place. When I was woven together in the depths of the earth, your eyes saw my unformed body" (Psalms 139:13–16).

You have known me from the moment I was conceived. You sorted through all the possible genes and chose the exact ones You wanted me to have so that I would glorify You. I cannot use my personality or physical make-up as an excuse for my weaknesses, because You have promised that Your grace is sufficient for me.

"All the days ordained for me were written in your book before one of them came to be" (Psalms 139:16).

You knew everything that would happen to me before I even took my first breath. You allowed both the good and the bad experiences so that I would grow into the person you planned for me to be.

"How precious to me are your thoughts, O God! How vast is the sum of them! Were I to count them, they would outnumber the grains of sand" (Psalms 139:17–18).

I am always on your Fatherly heart, which weeps for me when I am in pain and choose to shut You out.

"When I awake, I am still with you" (Psalms 139:18).

When I come to my senses, I realize that You were there all along. It was You who comforted me. It was You who carried me.

"Search me, O God, and know my heart; test me and know my anxious thoughts. See if there is any offensive way in me" (Psalms 139:23–24).

Show me the areas of my life that still need a touch from Your healing hands.

"Lead me in the way everlasting" (Psalms 139:24).

Cause me to be ever growing in my relationship with You.

"Search me, O God, and know my heart" (Psalms 139:23).

PART

Two

The Healing Journey

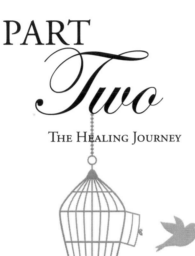

Arise, cry out in the night…
pour out your heart like water
in the presence of the Lord.
(Lamentations 2:19)

Heal me, O Lord, and I will be healed;
save me and I will be saved,
for you are the one I praise.
(Jeremiah 17:14)

CHAPTER

Eight

GRIEVING

Though you have made me see troubles, many and bitter,
you will restore my life again;
from the depths of the earth you will again bring me up.
You will increase my honor and comfort me once again.
(Psalms 71:20–21)

THE GRIEVING PROCESS

I TEND TO BE A VERY PRIVATE PERSON. WHEN I'M HURTING, I'M INCLINED to pull away from people and try to deal with my pain by myself. I take this time to pour out my heart to my Heavenly Father. That's good, but we also need to talk to some close friends or people we can trust. We were never intended to walk life's paths alone. We need each other. By not talking about my wounds, they moved inward where I buried them so well that even I didn't know they were there.

When my father died, and then shortly afterward my brother, the dam I had so carefully erected to hold back my emotions came crashing down. Suddenly I was no longer a private person; emotion flooded out of me everywhere I went.

I found the book *Understanding Grief* very helpful in accepting my grieving process:

> The majority of people tend to use the words "grieving" and "mourning" synonymously. An important distinction, however, exists between them. Individuals move toward healing not just by grieving, but through the process of mourning.[14]

The difference between grieving and mourning is that grieving is the inward expression of loss that we experience by ourselves, while mourning is the pouring out of our thoughts and feelings about our loss in public.

> Simply stated, grief is the composite of thoughts and feelings about a loss that you experience within yourself. In other words, grief is the internal meaning given to the experience of bereavement. In contrast, mourning is when you take the grief on the inside and express it outside of yourself. Another way of defining mourning is "grief gone public" or "sharing your grief outside yourself." Crying, talking about the person who died, or celebrating special anniversary dates of the person you loved are just a few examples of mourning.
>
> After someone loved dies, friends may encourage you to "keep your grief to yourself." The disastrous result is that all of your thoughts and feelings are neatly bottled up inside of you. A catalyst for healing, however; can only be created when you develop the courage to mourn publicly in the presence of understanding, caring persons who will not judge you. At times, of course, you will grieve alone, but expressing your grief outside yourself is necessary if you are to move forward in your grief journey.[15]

---

14 Wolfelt, Alan D. *Understanding Grief* (New York, NY: Brunner-Routledge, 1992), p. 8.
15 Ibid. pp. 8–9.

The grieving progression for each individual is unique to each personality but may have common stages or phases. "The concept of stages of grief was popularized in 1969 with the publication of Elisabeth Kubler-Ross' landmark text, 'On Death and Dying.'"[16]

The stages of grief are identified as—denial, anger, bargaining, depression, and acceptance.

- Denial—a period of shock; this isn't happening!
- Anger—why is this happening to me?
- Bargaining—if only I had or hadn't done it, this wouldn't have happened.
- Depression—this has happened and I'm helpless to change it.
- Acceptance—this has happened; it will change me forever, but I can go on.

However, these stages were never intended to be a hard and fast rule. They're only an example of what a grieving person may experience as she works toward healing. One may go through all the stages or phases of grief, or only some of them. She may experience each phase one at a time or several simultaneously.

For me, the important thing was not to try to force myself into someone else's mould of what they thought my grieving process should look like, but rather to allow myself to move through the grieving process naturally in whatever pattern my journey took me.

Our society often encourages prematurely moving away from grief instead of toward it. The result is that too many bereaved people either grieve in isolation or attempt to run away from their grief through various means.... Bereaved persons who continue to express grief outwardly are often viewed as "weak," "crazy," or "self-pitying." The subtle message is "shape up and get on with life." The reality is disturbing: far too many people view grief as something to be overcome rather than experienced...

16 Ibid. p. 9.

When your grief is ignored or minimized, you will feel further isolated in your journey. Ultimately, you will experience the onset of the "Am I going crazy?" syndrome. To mask or move away from your grief creates anxiety, confusion, and depression...[17]

My grieving process started off with denial, then plunged deep into depression, where I remained for over a year. My anger, at least that which was properly directed, didn't come about until I had done some healing.

My grieving journey could be described as a huge, circular rollercoaster. Its steep heights, sudden plunges, and twists and turns seemed to go round and round forever with no end in sight. Any given day could see me passing through one or all of the stages, and back again, in no particular order.

My difficulty was that I was grieving for many different reasons:

• The death of my father, with whom I had many unresolved issues.
• The death of my closest brother, who was the only person I had bonded with as a child.
• Thirty-five years of dammed-up emotion from an abusive childhood.
• The fact that I was burnt out from nine years in a difficult ministry.
• All my subsequent losses.

The situation set me up for an extremely complicated grieving journey. I felt imprisoned by my emotions. Again, through reading my Bible I discovered that the psalmist felt the same way.

Set me free from my prison, that I may praise your name. (Psalms 142:7)

---

17 Ibid. pp. 11–12.

After the second year of my healing journey, I began to notice that my highs weren't as extreme or unnatural and my lows weren't as deep or prolonged. I found that what had previously taken me eight to ten weeks to work through, I was now able to process in a period of one or two weeks. At times, the emotion would be so intense that I felt like I was starting back at the beginning of my healing journey; however, I was able to process the emotion much faster.

Grieving a loss can be compared to waves of the ocean during a storm. Sometimes the emotions are just as huge and terrifying.

From My Journal

I feel like a piece of driftwood lying on the warm sand, absorbing the loving caress of the sun. Suddenly, without warning, a giant wave reaches out and grabs me, throwing me into the deep, violent water.

The current is pulling me down. My lungs feel like they're going to burst from lack of oxygen. I struggle and fight against the undertow with all my might. I manage to reach the surface just long enough to take a breath of air before I'm pulled back under the fierce waves again.

I thrash about against the current as overwhelming fear springs up in my heart. Will I live through this or will I drown? I am so very tired now, it would feel good to just let go and let my life vanish. Suddenly, as quickly as it all began, I'm thrown back on the warm beach. I'm too exhausted to move, yet I whisper, "Thanks, Lord."

I'm lying on the beach, absorbing the warm sun, slowly drying out. It looks like there is hope for me. I think I'm going to live through this. But just as I begin to relax, another ferocious wave reaches out, overpowers me, and I'm tossed helplessly back into the tempestuous sea.

This tide of emotion has played over and over, day after day, week after week, month after month for a year and a half. Just when I feel I can no longer go on, there is hope, and when I think I will finally survive, I am thrown back into a torrent of emotion.

I'm too tired to fight anymore. I just want to relax and go under. Someone, something, has to pull me out, or I will drown.

I was not alone in my thoughts. The psalmist shared my feelings.

Save me, O God, for the waters have come up to my neck. I sink in the miry depths, where there is no foothold. I have come into the deep waters; the floods engulf me. I am worn out calling for help; my throat is parched. My eyes fail, looking for my God. (Psalms 69:1–3)

He reached down from on high and took hold of me; he drew me out of deep waters. He rescued me from my powerful enemy, from my foes [emotional wounds], who were too strong for me. They confronted me in the day of my disaster, but the Lord was my support. He brought me out into a spacious place; he rescued me because he delighted in me. (Psalms 18:16–19)

I waited patiently for the Lord; he turned to me and heard my cry. He lifted me out of the slimy pit, out of the mud and the mire; he set my feet on a rock and gave me a firm place to stand. He put a new song in my mouth, a hymn of praise to our God. Many will see and fear and put their trust in the Lord. (Psalms 40:1–3)

The day after writing this piece in my journal, I read:

Then he got into the boat and his disciples followed him. Without warning, a furious storm came up on the lake, so that the waves swept over the boat. But Jesus was sleeping. The disciples went and woke him, saying, "Lord, save us! We're going to drown!"
He replied, "You of little faith, why are you so afraid?" Then he got up and rebuked the winds and the waves, and it was completely calm.
The men were amazed and asked, "What kind of man is this? Even the winds and the waves obey him!" (Matthew 8:23–27)

I noted that the disciples fought the storm in their own strength until they knew they were beaten before asking for help. I also noticed that Jesus didn't calm the storm until His disciples asked Him to.

I was reminded of the many times I try to fight a storm on my own before giving the whole situation over to my Heavenly Father. I worry, fret, and fear sometimes for hours before I remember that I have a Good Shepherd who delights in taking care of me. It is then that I begin to pour out my heart to the one who loves me.

Trust in him at all times, [Grace];
pour out your heart to him,
for God is our refuge.
(Psalms 62:8)

I cry aloud to the Lord;
I lift up my voice to the Lord for mercy.
I pour out my complaint before him;
before him I tell my trouble.
(Psalms 142:1–2)

Arise, cry out in the night,
as the watches of the night begin;
pour out your heart like water
in the presence of the Lord.
(Lamentations 2:19)

The eyes of the Lord are on the righteous
and his ears are attentive to their cry…
The righteous cry out, and the Lord hears them;
he delivers them from all their troubles.
The Lord is close to the brokenhearted
and saves those who are crushed in spirit.
(Psalms 34: 15, 17–18)

REFLECTIONS ON PSALMS 23

"The Lord is my shepherd, I shall not be in want" (Psalms 23:1).

Father, You are my provider. I have everything I need. You know what I need before I even ask for it, but You delight in my coming to You so that You can shower me with Your blessings.

"He makes me lie down in green pastures, he leads me beside quiet waters" (Psalms 23:2).

You allow situations to come into my life so that I have to take time out to feed on Your Word and be reassured by You. You make me content and comfortable so that I am able to receive a restful sleep. You call me to take time away with You so that my spirit can be refreshed and I can experience Your peace.

"He restores my soul. He guides me in paths of righteousness for his name's sake" (Psalms 23:3).

When I'm down and unable to get back on my feet, You lift me up. You support and strengthen me until I am able to walk by Your side once again. You put Your desires into my heart and give me guidance to make healthy choices and decisions so that You are glorified in my life.

"Even though I walk through the valley of the shadow of death, I will fear no evil, for you are with me; your rod and your staff, they comfort me" (Psalms 23:4).

When my world falls apart and I fear the future, You calm my spirit and walk with me. Your presence removes all my fear and worry. You protect me and guide me so that I can avoid the potholes on my journey through this life.

"You prepare a table before me in the presence of my enemies. You anoint my head with oil; my cup overflows" (Psalms 23:5).

You allow me to have sweet fellowship with You even in the midst of the clamouring voices of my problems. You listen to my hurts and pour healing ointment on my wounds until my heart overflows with joy and praise so that others are touched by Your love.

"Surely goodness and love will follow me all the days of my life, and I will dwell in the house of the Lord forever" (Psalms 23:6).

My confidence is in You, Father, for You desire the very best for me and You bathe me in approval and acceptance my whole life through. And I will live in Your presence, both now and for eternity.

The God of All Comfort

This is why I weep and my eyes overflow with tears.
No one is near to comfort me, no one to restore my spirit.
My soul faints with longing for your salvation,
but I have put my hope in your word.
My eyes fail, looking for your promise;
I say, "When will you comfort me?"
My comfort in my suffering is this:
Your promise preserves my life.
I remember your ancient laws, O Lord,
and I find comfort in them.
If your law had not been my delight,
I would have perished in my affliction.

But now, this is what the Lord says—
he who created you,
he who formed, you:
"Fear not, for I have redeemed you;
I have summoned you by name; you are mine.
When you pass through the waters, I will be with you;
and when you pass through the rivers, they will not sweep over you.
When you walk through the fire, you will not be burned;
the flames will not set you ablaze.
Since you are precious and honoured in my sight,
and because I love you...
Do not be afraid, for I am with you.

As a mother comforts her child,
so will I comfort you; and you will be comforted...
For the Lord comforts his people
and will have compassion on his afflicted ones.
The Lord will surely comfort you
and will look with compassion on all your ruins;
He will make your deserts like Eden,
your wastelands like the garden of the Lord.
Joy and gladness will be found in you ,
thanksgiving and the sound of singing.[18]

---

18 Paraphrased from Lamentations 1:16; Psalms 119:81–82, 50, 52, 92; Isaiah 43:1–2, 4–5; Isaiah 49:13; Isaiah 51:3; Isaiah 66:13, and Isaiah 57:16, 18.

CHAPTER

Nine

BROKENNESS

What can I say for you?
With what can I compare you, O Daughter [Grace]?
To what can I liken you, that I may comfort you...?
Your wound is as deep as the sea.
Who can heal you [Grace]?
(Lamentations 2:13)

ALTHOUGH I WAS SLOWLY ACCEPTING GOD'S LOVE FOR ME, I HAD THIRTY-five years of pent-up emotion that had to be released if I was going to put my depression behind me. Like an infected boil that has to be lanced so the puss can be allowed to pour out, my festering emotions needed to be brought to the surface where they could be expressed.

Gradually, the Lord brought situations into my life that triggered flashbacks to the emotions of old wounds, causing my present emotions to flow.

From My Journal

I feel like crushed glass; like a crystal vase shattered into a thousand tiny pieces. It hurts so much. I didn't know anyone could be in this much pain and still be able to live. My whole being feels like it is crumbling. I hate it. I don't understand what is happening to me. I feel like it will never end.

Dear Jesus: I feel so broken, what has caused all this brokenness?

I began to reflect on what had taken place in my life to cause so much pain. There was the childhood sexual abuse at the hands of my father and others which robbed me of my childhood and purity and damaged my self-worth. Those experiences caused massive aftershocks. I was grieving the deaths of my brother and father. Their losses made me feel shattered.

But there was one other experience that had left me broken, a situation I had conveniently forgotten—or rather, hidden away. An area of my life that the Holy Spirit now put His finger on.

A two-year relationship I had with a young man while I was in high school had more wrong with it than the fact that he was an unbeliever. Add to that the reality that we had two different sets of morals, my craving affection, and all the time (too much) we spent on our own, and you have a recipe for disaster.

Eventually I did the thing I swore I would never do: I gave in to his advances. In one moment of weakness, I threw away what little self-respect I had managed to hold on to. I learned the hard lesson: sex outside the protection of marriage results in brokenness.

Suddenly my tempter became my accuser. *Now look what you've done. God will surely judge you now and He will never forgive you. You've ruined your life.*

So I watched my calendar, checking off the days of the month as they passed by—waiting, fearing, pleading, hoping, dreading the news that could forever change my life. I pleaded for God to forgive me and see fit to give me back my carefree high school days.

Only a young single girl, walking in my shoes, could understand the terror one lives through in these circumstances. Likewise, only that same person would understand the relief and joy when that moment finally arrived when I knew that my prayers had been heard and that I had escaped the shame and curse of becoming "an unwed mother," as we called it back then.

Eighteen months later, just days before that relationship came to an end, I walked into the same trap and lived the same nightmare all over again.

I am reminded of an illustration I once read. The purpose of the illustration was to demonstrate to a youth group the importance of saving sex until marriage.

Take a piece of red construction paper and write a girl's name on it. For example, "Grace." Then use some white glue to bond it to a piece of blue construction paper with a boy's name on it—let's say, "Dave." Set it aside to dry. Take the dried bonded paper and try to separate the two pieces. The result will be that the red paper will come away with blue pieces of paper stuck to it and the blue paper will retain some of the red paper.

The Bible means it when it says that "the two become one flesh." During the act of sex, the souls of the two individuals bond together, so that when the relationship is over, the souls of the two people have to be torn from each other, resulting in brokenness and the carrying away of particles of each other's soul. That's why breaking up with someone with whom there has been a sexual relationship is more painful than one that has not advanced that far. As more partners are added, the bond typically becomes weaker and separation less painful.

Now, if you take the red paper and bond it to a piece of yellow paper and you take the blue paper and bond it to a piece of orange paper, then try to separate them, you will find more particles left behind. The red paper will now contain pieces of blue and yellow paper and the blue paper will hold pieces of both red and orange paper. The more sexual partners a person has, the more fragments of his or her soul will be torn away and exchanged with the other individuals. This is true whether the sexual act was with consent or whether it was forced.

I have heard it said that when two people sleep together, they are actually bringing all their previous partners into the relationship with them. The bond that takes place during the act of sex is referred to by some writers as "alien bonding." Barbara Wilson refers to this bonding as "the invisible bond" in her books, *The Invisible Bond*[19] and *Kiss Me Again*.[20] In these books, Barbara walks the reader step by step toward healing.

The problem with these premarital bonds is that they prevent the individuals from bonding well to their partner when they do eventually marry. Consequently, their desired emotional intimacy continuously eludes them. When you glue two objects together, you need both surfaces to be clean and smooth for optimal bonding to take place. So it only makes sense that when two people come together with scarred souls, they will have difficulty establishing a healthy bond. As a result, there is often not enough tenaciousness in the relationship to enable the marriage to endure the difficult times.

Another dilemma with premarital sexual relationships, which is also true of abuse victims, is that once a soul has been bonded to multiple partners, it often craves more sexual partners so that even though a person is happily married, he or she may struggle with lust, which often leads to long-term bondage, sexual addictions, and/or an affair.

> *Flee from sexual immorality.*
> *All other sins a man commits are outside his body,*
> *but he who sins sexually sins against his own body.*
> (1 Corinthians 6:18)

From My Journal

Jesus, will I ever be whole again? Will I ever awaken in the morning and be filled with joy at the thought of greeting a new day? Jesus, could you possibly take all these fragmented pieces of my shattered life and put them back together again?

---

19 Wilson, Barbara. *The Invisible Bond* (Colorado Springs, CO: Multnomah Books, 2006).
20 Wilson, Barbara. *Kiss Me Again* (Colorado Springs, CO: Multnomah Books, 2009).

I looked for an answer in Scripture and found that David expressed the same feelings: *"I have become like broken pottery"* (Psalms 31:12). I looked for other references to pottery and read about broken pottery that is not thrown away, but remade.

"So I went down to the potter's house, and I saw him working at the wheel. But the pot he was shaping from the clay was marred in his hands; so the potter formed it into another pot, shaping it as seemed best to him… [Grace], can I not do with you as this potter does?" declares the Lord. "Like clay in the hand of the potter, so are you in my hand, [Grace]." (Jeremiah 18:3–4, 6)

O Lord, you are our Father. We are the clay, you are the potter; we are all the work of your hand. (Isaiah 64:8)

The Lord will fulfill his purpose for me, your love, O Lord, endures forever—do not abandon the works of your hands. (Psalms 138:8)

I read about God's promises to heal me.

I will restore you to health and heal your wounds, declares the Lord. (Jeremiah 30:17)

He heals the brokenhearted and binds up their wounds. (Psalms 147:3)

The Lord is close to the brokenhearted and saves those who are crushed in spirit. (Psalms 34:18)

A prophecy of the Messiah states:

The Lord has anointed me to preach good news to the poor. He has sent me to bind up the brokenhearted, to proclaim freedom for the captives and release from darkness for the prisoners… to comfort all who mourn, and provide for those who grieve… to bestow on them a crown of beauty instead of ashes, the oil of gladness instead of mourning, and a garment of praise instead of a spirit of despair. They will be called oaks of righteousness, a planting of the Lord for the display of his splendour. (Isaiah 61:1–3)

Come to me,
all you who are weary and burdened,
and I will give you rest.
Take my yoke upon you
and learn from me,
for I am gentle
and humble in heart,
and you will find rest for your souls.
For my yoke is easy and my burden is light.
(Matthew 11:28-30)

Healing Hands

I was a shattered crystal vase
lying there in pain.
I had such very little hope
of being whole again.

I laid in a thousand fragments
crushed beyond repair.
You tenderly gathered up each piece
and glued with loving-care.

Your hands, they never tired.
Your comfort never ceased,
until the crystal vase once more
stood there without a crease.

Jesus, I'm truly grateful.
My God I offer praise.
For through Your loving nail-pierced hands
You've healed this broken vase.

 CHAPTER
Ten

DEPRESSION

Why, O Lord, do you stand far off?
Why do you hide yourself
in times of trouble?
(Psalms 10:1)

From My Journal

My counsellor tells me that my depression is the result of turning my intense emotions inward. Exhaustion from burnout kept me from having the energy to process my feelings of grief over losing my father and brother. Consequently, my emotions became suppressed. My problem is not that I have a mental illness but rather internalized grief. Add to that suicidal thoughts planted in my mind by Satan and the result is deep, deep depression.

I HAD MANY DAYS WHEN MY DEPRESSION WAS SO DEEP THAT JUST PUTTING one foot in front of the other to walk across the floor took tremendous concentration. I couldn't eat or sleep for days on end and dropped thirty pounds in three weeks. I resembled a walking skeleton. Later, after I was well, someone commented that even when I smiled, my eyes looked dead.

Again, I looked for someone I could identify with in Scripture and found several individuals.

DAVID

David referred to his anguished emotions in a number of his Psalms.

Give me relief from my distress; be merciful to me and hear my prayer. (Psalms 4:1)

Give ear to my words, O Lord, consider my sighing. Listen to my cry for help. (Psalms 5:1–2)

Be merciful to me, Lord, for I am faint; O Lord, heal me for my bones are in agony. My soul is in anguish. How long, O Lord, how long?... I am worn out from groaning; all night long I flood my bed with weeping and drench my couch with tears. My eyes grow weak with sorrow... (Psalms 6:2–3, 6–7)

Why, O Lord, do you stand far off? Why do you hide yourself in times of trouble? (Psalms 10:1)

How long, O Lord? Will you forget me forever? How long will you hide your face from me? How long must I wrestle with my thoughts and every day have sorrow in my heart? How long will my enemy [emotional scars] triumph over me? Look on me and answer me, O Lord my God. Give light to my eyes, or I will sleep in death. (Psalms 13:1–3)

My thoughts trouble me and I am distraught... My heart is in anguish within me. (Psalms 55:2, 4)

For my soul is full of trouble and my life draws near the grave. I am counted among those who go down to the pit; I am like a man without strength. You have put me in the lowest pit, in the darkest depths. (Psalms 88:3–4, 6)

ELIJAH

Elijah dropped into depression right after his great victory over the prophets of Baal in 1 Kings 18:16–45. In 1 Kings 19:1–16, we read of Elijah's depression.

Elijah was afraid and ran for his life. (1Kings 19:3)

He left his servant... [and] went a day's journey into the desert. (1Kings 19:3–4)

He came to a broom tree, sat under it and prayed that he might die. "I have had enough, Lord," he said. "Take my life..." (1Kings 19:4)

Then he lay down under the tree and fell asleep [being exhausted from ministry]. (1Kings 19:5)

All at once an angel touched him and said, "Get up and eat." [He had gone without food]. He looked around, and there by his head was a cake of bread baked over hot coals, and a jar of water. He ate and drank and then lay down again. (1Kings 19:5–6)

The angel of the Lord came back a second time and touched him and said, "Get up and eat, for the journey is too much for you." So he got up and ate and drank. Strengthened by that food, he traveled forty days and forty nights until he reached Horeb, the mountain

of God. There he went into a cave and spent the night. (1Kings
19:7–9)

There in the cave, the Lord met with Elijah and comforted him. The
Lord gave him a job to do, then told him, *"Go back the way you came"*
(1Kings 19:15). I wonder, as Elijah walked back the way he came, as he
reached each landmark, if God brought back to his memory the various
emotions he had experienced on his earlier journey, showing him how
He had provided for him?

Elijah ran away when he got frightened and depressed. I could
identify with him, as I often felt like running away. I dreamed of getting
on a train and heading west. I don't know what I planned on doing
when I reached my destination, but I repeatedly had the overwhelming
urge to run from my pain. Fortunately, I never had enough money for
a ticket.

Once again, I found comfort in the Psalms of David.

*My heart is in anguish within me… Fear and trembling have beset
me; horror has overwhelmed me. I said, "Oh, that I had the wings
of a dove! I would fly away and be at rest—I would flee far away
and stay in the desert… I would hurry to my place of shelter, far
from the tempest and storm."* (Psalms 55:4–8)

PETER

Jesus also brought Peter back the way he came to enable him to heal.
The night that Jesus was arrested, Peter stood around a charcoal fire,
warming himself with the servants. It was at that fire that Peter denied
knowing Jesus three times (John 18:15–27). In Luke 22:61, we read that
right after Peter denied knowing Jesus the third time, the rooster crowed
and *"the Lord turned and looked straight at Peter."*

After His resurrection, Jesus met the disciples on the shore where
He had a charcoal fire burning. I'm sure that as he ate his breakfast,
Peter thought about the last time Jesus had looked at him across a fire,

immediately after Peter had denied knowing his Lord three times. Jesus lovingly took this opportunity to restore their relationship by asking, three times, "Peter, do you love me?" Jesus restored him and then gave him a ministry, saying, *"Feed my sheep"* (John 21:9, 15–17).

JESUS

David Seamands, in his book *Healing for Damaged Emotions*, gives a commentary on the hours leading up to Jesus' trial.

Jesus suffered extensive emotional pain in the garden of Gethsemane.

To understand what it cost the Saviour to be our Healer, we need to walk with Him through His passion and suffering, as shown in the Gospels... Come with me now into the Garden of Gethsemane. Discover what it cost our Saviour to be Emmanuel, God with us. Listen to His prayers. Can you hear them, as if for the first time? He *"began to be sorrowful and very heavy. Then saith he unto them, 'My soul is exceeding sorrowful, even unto death'"* (Matthew 26:37–38, KJV).

Wait a minute, Jesus. What did You say? *"My soul is exceeding sorrowful, even unto death"*? Do You mean to say that You experienced such feelings, such emotions and pain in that wretched hour, that You even wanted to die? Do You mean to say, Lord, You understand when I am so depressed that I no longer want to live?...

"Peter, what, could ye not watch with Me for one hour?" (Matthew 26:40, KJV). Three times He implored His friends, but to no avail. Finally, *"all the disciples forsook Him, and fled"* (Matthew 26:56, KJV).

If you have battled terrible loneliness, or pathological emptiness, if you have experienced the blackest bouts of depression, you know that when you are in the pits, the hardest thing to do is to pray, because you do not feel God's presence. I want to assure you that He knows, He understands, He feels your infirmity. He shares all your feelings because He has been through them.[21]

Like Elijah and Peter, I had to go back the way I came and revisit my traumas and wounded emotions so that I could heal. And then the Lord gave me a job to do: help other wounded people to find their way through their own wilderness journey.

As I began to revisit my childhood wounds and release the emotions they raised, my depression gradually lifted and I began to feel some hope for my future.

Those who hope in me
will not be disappointed.
(Isaiah 49:23)

May the God of hope
fill you with all joy and peace
as you trust in him,
so that you may overflow with hope
by the power of the Holy Spirit.
(Romans 15:13)

---

21 Seamands, David A. *Healing for Damaged Emotions* (Colorado Springs, CO: Chariot Victor Publishing, 1991), pp. 41–42.

Hope in God

Why are you downcast, O my soul? Why so disturbed within me?
Put your hope in God, for I will yet praise him,
my Saviour and my God.
Hope deferred makes the heart, sick.

Yet this I call to mind and therefore I have hope:
Because of the Lord's great love we are not consumed,
for his compassions never fail.
They are new every morning; great is your faithfulness.
The Lord is good to those whose hope is in him.

For everything that was written in the past
was written to teach us, so that through endurance
and the encouragement of the scriptures we might have hope.

Those who hope in the Lord will renew their strength.
They will soar on wings like eagles; they will run and not grow weary,
they will walk and not be faint.
No one whose hope is in you will ever be put to shame.

"For I know the plans I have for you," declares the Lord,
"plans to prosper you and not to harm you,
plans to give you hope and a future."

May the God of hope, fill you with all joy and peace,
as you trust in him,
so that you may overflow with hope by the power of the Holy Spirit.
Find rest, O my soul, in God alone;
my hope comes from him.[22]

---

22 Paraphrased from Psalms 42:5; Proverbs 13:12; Lamentations 3:21–23, 25;
Romans 15:4; Isaiah 40:31; Psalms 25:3; Jeremiah 29:11; Romans 15:13; and
Psalms 62:5.

 CHAPTER

Eleven

CONFUSION

In my anguish
I cried to the Lord,
and he answered
by setting me free.
(Psalms 118:5)

From My Journal

I am told that one of the first steps to healing is to allow yourself to feel your real feelings. Yet some of my friends say, "Why are you digging up past feelings and experiences? It's just making you feel worse. Stop feeling sorry for yourself. This will go on as long as you want it to. What's done is done. It's covered in the blood of Christ; put it behind you and move on in your life." But I can't!

Present experiences seem to tap into an immense reservoir of emotion and I don't know how to stop it. When something upsets me, I don't just cry, I sob. I'm never in need of just a little affection, I feel like I'm going to die from loneliness. When something ticks me off, I'm not just a little angry; I fly into a fit of rage that erupts like a volcano looking to kill.

One day when I got home from church, I said to my husband, "If one more person pats me on the arm and says, 'Just hold on to the Lord, dear. He'll never give you more than you are able to bear,' I'm going to take off my shoe and pound her on the head until she cries out in pain and then I'll pat her on the arm and say, 'Just hold on to the Lord, dear. He'll never give you more than you are able to bear.'"

I've had people imply that if I were reading my Bible, I wouldn't be depressed. But I read my Bible every day, for hours every day. I've had people say that real believers don't get depressed, implying that there must be something lacking in my faith.

From My Journal

Dear Jesus: I'm sorry if my faith is too small or if I'm drowning in self-pity. I don't mean to say that Your blood isn't strong enough to wipe away my wounds, but I hurt so much. I'm so confused. Why can't I put my wounds behind me? Please lead me in Your path for my healing.

"For I know the plans I have for you, [Grace]," declares the Lord, "plans to prosper you [Grace] and not to harm you; plans to give you hope and a future." (Jeremiah 29:11)

I am the Lord your God, who teaches you what is best for you, [Grace,] who directs you in the way you should go. (Isaiah 48:17)

I will lead [Grace] by ways [she has] not known, along unfamiliar paths I will guide [her]; I will turn the darkness into light before [her] and make the rough places smooth. These are the things I will do; I will not forsake [Grace]. (Isaiah 42:16)

From My Journal

My counsellor tells me that my confusion is caused from "feeling flashbacks." When more emotion is felt than what the circumstances call for, I am experiencing childhood emotions that were unable to be expressed when I was a child. Or they could be emotions from a previous wound that hasn't been dealt with.

Feeling flashbacks are somewhat like visual flashbacks, but you don't see anything happening. You have feelings, but you don't know what's causing them or where they're coming from. You go to bed at night feeling normal and in the morning you wake up severely depressed or angry or lonely. You can be going about your day when suddenly a powerful emotion comes over you. There's no explanation for it and you begin to think that you're going crazy.

Many times, I actually felt like a child. When I began connecting my intense emotions with childhood suffering, I realized that I often felt the age I had been when that trauma took place.

After my counsellor explained "feeling flashbacks" to me, I would take some time out when this happened and go to my Heavenly Father, asking Him to show me where the emotion was coming from. Usually it was something that had happened a day or two previously which triggered pain from past wounds. My Heavenly Father would take my memory back to where I had been wounded and comfort me while I expressed the appropriate emotion.

When I was a child,
I talked like a child,
I thought like a child,
I reasoned like a child.
When I became a man,
I put away childish things.
(1 Corinthians 13:11)

You Knew the Anguish of My Soul

If only my anguish could be weighed
and all my misery be placed on the scales!
It would surely outweigh the sand of the seas.
No wonder my words have been impetuous.

I said, "I will watch my ways and keep my tongue from sin;
I will put a muzzle on my mouth."
But when I was silent and still, my anguish increased.
Therefore I will not keep silent.
I will speak out in the anguish of my spirit,
I will complain in the bitterness of my soul.

Be merciful to me, Lord, for I am faint.
O Lord, heal me, for my bones are in agony.
My soul is in anguish.
How long, O Lord, how long?
Turn, O Lord, and deliver me.
Save me because of your unfailing love.

In my anguish I cried to the Lord,
and he answered by setting me free.
I will be glad and rejoice in your love,
for you saw my affliction
and knew the anguish of my soul.
You have not handed me over to the enemy
but have set my feet in a spacious place.[23]

---

23 Paraphrased from Job 6:2–3; Psalms 39:1–2; Job 7: 11; Psalms 6:2-4; Psalms 118:5; and Psalms 31:7–8.

CHAPTER
Twelve

WORTHLESSNESS

O Lord, how long will you look on?
Rescue my life from these ravages,
my precious life from these lions.
(Psalms 35:17)

I CARRIED AROUND A FOREBODING SENSE OF WORTHLESSNESS THAT never really went away. It would often go into hiding when I was with people, but once on my own again it wasn't long in returning.

One day, when I was reading my Bible, I read, *"O Lord, how long will you look on? Rescue my life from their ravages, my precious life from these lions"* (Psalms 35:17). I wrote in the margin of my Bible, "Is my life precious? Do I have value?" I also noted that my lions were the many emotional wounds I had endured along the way in growing up.

Another day I found a verse that showed me how God felt about my value:

For you are a people holy to the Lord your God. The Lord your God has chosen you out of all the peoples on the face of the earth to be his people, his treasured possession. (Deuteronomy 7:6)

I read it over and over and over again. I couldn't believe my eyes. I began to sob uncontrollably. No one had ever told me before that I had value. Yet here was the creator of the universe, telling me that I was *"his treasured possession."* I was valuable not because of what I did or who I was, but whose I was. God had chosen me, and His signature of ownership on my life made all the difference in the world.

"The Lord your God has chosen you out of all the peoples on the face of the earth..." (Deuteronomy 7:6)

I could relate to what "chosen" meant. When we got our first dog, we went to a dog pound and looked at all the dogs that were available. We went from cage to cage, not really impressed with anything we saw, until suddenly there she was. She was beautiful; she was perfect. There, looking up at us and wagging her little tail, was a taffy-coloured terrier poodle. She was exactly what we had prayed for. We chose Buffy. Out of all the dogs we saw that day, Buffy was chosen.

"...to be his people..." (Deuteronomy 7:6)

We paid for Buffy, set her free from her cage, put her on a leash to keep her safe while we walked her to the car, took her home, and adopted her into our family. Buffy was our dog; she belonged to us and we loved her. That's what God did for me. He paid for me. He set me free from bondage. He gave me guidelines to live by for my own protection. He adopted me into His family and He loves me.

"...his treasured possession" (Deuteronomy 7:6).

The value of an object is determined by the price that someone is willing to pay for it. I was bought with the precious blood of Jesus.

Another verse came to mind:

For you know that it was not with perishable things such as silver or gold that you were redeemed from the empty way of life handed down to you from your forefathers, but with the precious blood of Christ, a lamb without blemish or defect. (1 Peter 1:18–19)

"It was not with perishable things such as silver or gold that [I was] redeemed" (1 Peter 1:18).

This is true because such things depreciate and appreciate in value according to the present economy, a temporary effect.

"[I was] redeemed from the empty way of life handed down to me from my forefathers…" (1 Peter 1:18).

I was redeemed from their selfishness, alcoholism, violence, and abuse.

"…with the precious blood of Christ [that is priceless and never depreciates], a lamb without blemish or defect" (1 Peter 1:19).

I was redeemed from my feelings of worthlessness, emptiness, and brokenness.

I was bought with the priceless, precious blood of Christ. Silver and gold weren't enough to purchase me. It took the death of the perfect Son of God to purchase my forgiveness and make me God's child. I am priceless! I was and ever shall be God's treasured possession.

GOD EXCHANGED—

His preciousness, for my worthlessness,
His perfect wholeness, for my brokenness,
His fullness, for my emptiness,
His strength, for my weakness,
His peace, for my anxiety and fears,
His comfort and healing, for my wounds,
His presence, for my loneliness,
His joy, for my sorrow,
and His purity, for the filth of my abuse.

Recently I entered the words "treasured possession" into Biblegateway. com and discovered that God refers to His people as his "treasured possession" six times in the Old Testament.

Awake, awake, [Grace],
clothe yourself with strength.
Put on your garments of splendor...
Shake off your dust;
rise up...
Free yourself from the chains on your neck,
O captive daughter...
Your were sold for nothing,
and without money
you will be redeemed.
(Isaiah 52:1-3)

IS MY LIFE PRECIOUS?
O Lord, how long will you look on?
Rescue my life from these ravages,
my precious life from these lions.

I AM CREATED
This is what the Lord says—
he who created you,
he who formed you,
you who are called by my name,
whom I created for my glory,
whom I formed and made."

I AM CALLED BY NAME
I have summoned you by name;
you are mine—

I AM PRECIOUS; I AM LOVED
Since you are precious and honored in my sight,
and because I love you,
I will give men in exchange for you,
and people in exchange for your life.

I AM CHOSEN; I AM TREASURED
I took you from the ends of the earth,
from its farthest corners I called you.
I said, 'You are my servant';
I have chosen you and have not rejected you.
For you are a people holy to the Lord your God.
The Lord your God has chosen you
out of all the peoples on the face of the earth
to be his people,
his treasured possession.

I AM REDEEMED; I AM BOUGHT; I AM PRECIOUS
No man can redeem the life of another
or give to God a ransom for him—
the ransom for a life is costly,
no payment is ever enough—
Fear not, for I have redeemed you.
For you know that it was not with perishable things
such as silver or gold
that you were redeemed from the empty way of life
handed down to you from your forefathers,
but with the precious blood of Christ,
a lamb without blemish or defect.

I AM GOD'S TEMPLE
Do you not know
that your body is a temple of the Holy Spirit,
who is in you,
whom you have received from God?
You are not your own;
you were bought at a price.
Therefore honor God with your body.
Within your temple, O God,
I meditate on your unfailing love.

I AM GOD'S PROJECT
Being confident of this,
that he who began a good work in you
will carry it on to completion
until the day of Christ Jesus.
"For I know the plans I have for you,"
declares the Lord,
"plans to prosper you and not to harm you,
plans to give you hope and a future."

I AM GOD'S MASTERPIECE; I AM VALUABLE

For you created my inmost being;
you, yourself, knit me together in my mother's womb.
I praise you because I am fearfully and wonderfully made;
your works are wonderful,
I know that full well.
My frame was not hidden from you
when I was made in the secret place.
When I was woven together in the depths of the earth,
your eyes saw my unformed body.
All the days ordained for me
were written in your book
before one of them came to be.
How precious are your thoughts of me, O God!
How vast is the sum of them!
Were I to count them, they would outnumber the grains of sand.
When I awake, I am still with you.

I AM TRANSFORMED

The Lord will fulfill his purpose for me;
your love, O Lord, endures forever—
do not abandon the works of your hands.
And we, who with unveiled faces
all reflect the Lord's glory,
are being transformed into his likeness
with ever-increasing glory.
And I—in righteousness
I will see your face;
When I awake in heaven,
I will be satisfied with what you have done in my life
when seeing your likeness in me.[24]

---

24 Paraphrased from Psalm 35:17; Isaiah 43:1, 7, 4; Isaiah 41:9; Deuteronomy 7:6; Psalm 49:7, 8; Isaiah 43:4;1 Peter 1:18, 19; 1 Corinthians 6:19, 20; Philippians 1:6; Jeremiah 29:11; Psalm 139:13–18; Psalm 138:8; Psalm 48:9; 2 Corinthians 3:18; and Psalm 17:15.

 CHAPTER
Thirteen

LONELINESS

*In all their distress
he too was distressed…
In his love and mercy
he redeemed them;
he lifted them up
and carried them.*
(Isaiah 63:9)

I HAD BEEN PLAGUED ALL MY LIFE BY LONELINESS. ONE DAY, I ASKED MY
Heavenly Father, "Where does my loneliness come from?" As I quieted
my heart and allowed the Lord to comfort me through His Word, He
began to show me where my loneliness was rooted.

During the first eighteen months of my life, our family went
through four major crises. Three of my siblings became deathly ill with
unrelated life-threatening illnesses. One was not expected to live more
than two years, but she was miraculously healed and is still living today;
the other two spent extensive time in Sick Kid's Hospital in Toronto, but
eventually recovered. The fourth crisis involved the teenage pregnancy of
my oldest sister, who gave birth when she was only sixteen years of age.

I'm sure my mother wanted to take good care of me, but she was just too weary and worn out to do the job well.

The Lord gave me a vision of a newborn baby lying with a bottle propped up on a pillow, signifying that this was how I was often feed. Loneliness has an opportunity to take root when a child isn't cuddled frequently, often producing promiscuity when the child reaches his or her teen years.

People are created for relationship and physical affection, which is a very important part of interaction; however, we weren't a family that expressed physical affection. Nor were we a family that shared deeply. Our emotions were hidden by jokes; serious matters weren't discussed, at least not in a healthy way. Crises were not explained to the children but instead treated as though they never happened.

We all wore masks to hide our loneliness and fear. We lived the empty way of life handed down to us from our forefathers. Consequently, I never bonded with my mother or any other member of my family except my one brother, who had recently died.

I don't remember ever being hugged by either of my parents. I'm sure it is because their parents never hugged them, either. You can't take blood from a stone. If it's not in you to give, how can you? Physical affection—what is that?

From the time I conceived my first child, I prayed that God would teach me to be a good parent, and over the years the Lord has brought many people and circumstances into my life as a means of answering my prayers.

Lia, a Spanish woman who worked with me in the Ontario Housing Ministry, began to reach out and pull me into a hug. I responded the way I always did to female affection… I stiffened. She said, "You're very cold, aren't you?" But she never gave up on me and gradually I began to warm to her affection. God also used a husband and wife doctor team who treated me throughout my healing process. They would hug me every time they saw me. They did much to teach me about healthy affection.

The third individual was Joanne, a newly converted prostitute whom I was discipling. She had been sending her two daughters to our Sunday

School in the apartment building, and during a short time spent in jail for a misdemeanour she gave her life to the Lord. While I taught her how to walk in her new faith, she taught me how to first receive, and then give, affection.

I found examples in Scripture of Jesus reaching out and touching people. Jesus touched the children. He washed the disciples' feet. He put mud on a blind man's eyes. Jesus often touched the people He healed, including the lepers whom nobody touched because they were contagious and unclean.

Years later, I picked up a book entitled *The Five Love Languages of Children*.[25] The book explains that there are five basic ways in which people are able to feel loved. Each person has one particular love language that speaks loudest to them. The five love languages are:

- Physical Touch
- Words of Affirmation
- Quality Time
- Gifts
- Acts of Service

As I read through this book, I began to see more reasons as to why I felt lonely and of no value. My love language had never been spoken to me as a child, and neither were any of the other love languages. But my Heavenly Father, in His love for me, brought people into my life who showed me physical affection, spoke life into me with their words of affirmation, spent one-on-one time with me, gave me little trinkets that showed they cared about me, and served me by providing practical help.

One day as I studied Luke 15:11-24, about the prodigal son, I noted that all of these love languages were expressed by the father.

When he came to his senses, he said... "I will set out and go back to my father and say to him: Father, I have sinned against heaven and against you. I am no longer worthy to be called your son; make

---

25 Chapman, Gary and Ross Campbell. *The Five Love Languages of Children* (United Kingdom: Alpha, 1998).

me like one of your hired men." So he got up and went to his father. But while he was still a long way off, his father saw him and was filled with compassion for him; he ran to his son, threw his arms around him and kissed him. The son said to him, "Father, I have sinned against heaven and against you. I am no longer worthy to be called your son." But the father said to his servants, "Quick! Bring the best robe and put it on him. Put a ring on his finger and sandals on his feet. Bring the fattened calf and kill it. Let's have a feast and celebrate. For this son of mine was dead and is alive again; he was lost and is found." So they began to celebrate" (Luke 15:17–24).

- Physical Touch: *"He ran to his son, threw his arms around him and kissed him"* (Luke 15:20).
- Words of Affirmation: *"This son of mine* [he will not be a servant, he is my son] *"* (Luke 15:24).
- Quality Time: The son was to be seated in the position of honour, next to his father.
- Gifts: *"Put a ring on his finger and sandals on his feet"* (Luke 15:22).
- Acts of Service: *"Bring the fattened calf and kill it. Let's have a feast and celebrate"* (Luke 15:23).

My Heavenly Father speaks all five of the love languages to me. He is with me and comforts me in all of my distress. He surrounds me with His love and calms my heart when I am afraid. He speaks words of acceptance to me and calls me His beloved daughter. He enjoys fellowship with me and enters into communion with me. He gives healing and restoration to my soul. He provides for all my needs— spiritually, emotionally, and physically.

> *The Lord your God is with you [Grace],*
> *he is mighty to save.*
> *He will take great delight in you [Grace],*
> *he will quiet you with his love,*
> *he will rejoice over you [Grace] with singing.*

The sorrows for the appointed feasts
I will remove from you [Grace];
they are a burden and a reproach to you.
(Zephaniah 3:17–18)

God's Affection

Let the beloved of the Lord rest secure in him,
for he shields her all day long,
and the one the Lord loves
rests between his shoulders.
He tends his flock like a shepherd:
He gathers the lambs in his arms
and carries them close to his heart.
In all their distress he too was distressed...
In his love and mercy he redeemed them;
he lifted them up and carried them.

As a loving mother comforts her child,
so will I comfort you;
and you will be comforted.
I will take great delight in you.
I will quiet you with my love.
I will rejoice over you with singing.

In the desert the Lord your God carried you,
as a father carries his son,
all the way you went
until you reached this place.
In a desert land he found you,
in a barren and howling waste.
He shielded you and cared for you;
he guarded you as the apple of his eye,
like an eagle that stirs up its nest
and hovers over its young,
that spreads its wings to catch them
and carries them on its pinions.

And he took the children in his arms,
put his hands on them and blessed them.[26]

---

26 Paraphrased from Deuteronomy 33:12; Isaiah 40:11; Isaiah 63:9; Isaiah 66:13; Zephaniah 3:17; Deuteronomy 1:31; Deuteronomy 32:10-11; and Mark 10:16.

CHAPTER Fourteen

ANGER, RAGE, HATRED

O Lord, you took up my case;
you redeemed my life.
You have seen, O Lord,
the wrong done to me.
(Lamentations 3:58, 59)

THE CHANGE IN ME WAS FRIGHTENING. IN FACT, I BEGAN TO THINK I was going crazy. I had gone from being a mild-mannered person who showed very little emotion to one whose emotions flowed out everywhere I went. At times, it was like a dam bursting open and spewing out putrid water.

Throughout my healing process, I attended several support groups for survivors. The groups consisted of six to eight women of all ages and walks of life. In these groups, I learned that I wasn't alone in my experiences and emotional damage. There were always two or three women in each group who I was able to identify with.

One woman in the support group described the feeling of being out of control with intense anger whenever someone tried to overpower her emotionally. Through the development of the discussion, she shared that she had never been allowed to show any anger as a child. Expressing anger would have meant even greater pain. As a result, she was now experiencing flashbacks to the anger she had felt as a child but hadn't been allowed to express. I could definitely identify with her situation. Now, years later in a support group, all this anger and hatred began to bubble to the surface.

One evening in our support group opening statements, I said, "Why did God put so many men on one little planet?"

The group coordinator responded with, "Yes, fifty percent does seem rather high, doesn't it?" To which the rest of the group applauded.

Later in the session, I shared the experience I'd had while walking my dog in the park the previous week. I had just brought Buffy home from the pound three weeks earlier and was uninformed as to what happens when you walk a female dog that is in heat. Within minutes, I was surrounded by six male dogs. I picked my little dog up and held her while they circled me, trying to jump up and have their way with her. The entire pack followed me home.

This experience threw me into a feeling flashback as I paralleled what it felt like to walk down the street and have men whistle, honk their horn, or worse, say something disgusting like, "Honey, you can share my bed anytime." Being ogled like that made me feel like recycled trash. It reinforced the belief that my only value was sexual. Tears stung my eyes as I said that all I had ever wanted was for men to be able to look beyond my blond hair, blue eyes, and slim figure to see who I am inside. When I finished telling my story, other members of the group shared their concerns on the topic.

After sessions like this, I would go home enraged at men for the way they treat women. Some would say that these sessions weren't good for me, but they were. When a survivor isn't able to feel her own pain or anger, she is frequently able to experience it through another person's story. This helps to bring her own emotions to the surface, so that they can be expressed and healing can take place.

As part of my healing work, I would take my concerns to prayer. Suddenly, I blurted out, "Why do men have to be such dogs, always looking for an opportunity?" Gradually my rage simmered down enough to hear the Holy Spirit's voice within me,

"Now Grace, men are not the enemy. Satan is. He hates you and wants to destroy you."

For our struggle is not against flesh and blood, but… against the powers of this dark world and against the spiritual forces of evil in the heavenly realms. (Ephesians 6:12)

Most of these men aren't bad men. They're similarly suffering from the aftermath of childhood trauma. They are wounded, and wounded people wound other people.

Up to this point in my healing process, I was unable to get in touch with my anger toward my perpetrators. I had no problem, however, expressing an abundance of anger at my husband and men in general. In fact, I walked around my house days on end, ranting and raving about all the disgusting men in the world. I think there were times when my husband feared for his life. Actually, I think he slept with one eye open.

In one of my fits of rage, I retorted to my husband, "The next relationship I have is going to be with a woman." I may not have been too serious with that statement, but given the intense hatred I had for men and the instability of my marriage at the time, but for the grace of God, that may very well have been my future.

In contrast, I was unable to feel any anger at those who had caused me so much devastation. I loved those who had abused me, and holding them responsible for what they had done to me would mean that I'd have to accept that they didn't love me at all.

Much of the process of getting in touch with my anger was dealt with as I wrote in my journal. My counsellor had given me assignments to write letters to those who had hurt me as a means of expressing my emotions. These letters were never intended to be mailed; they were simply for the benefit of releasing emotions. It took a very long time to get to the place where I could accept that I hadn't been loved by these people and consequently be able to experience, process, and then release my anger at those who had brought so much destruction into my life.

> *In your anger do not sin;*
> *when you are on your beds,*
> *search your hearts and be silent.*
> [Ask yourself, "Why am I angry?"]
> (Psalms 4:4)

He Speaks to Me in My Affliction

He does not ignore the cry of the afflicted.
But those who suffer, he delivers in their suffering.
He speaks to them in their affliction.
In all their distress, he too, was distressed…
In his love and mercy he redeemed them;
He lifted them up and carried them…

For he tends his flock like a shepherd:
He gathers the lambs in his arms
and carries them close to his heart…
Let the beloved of the Lord rest secure in him,
for he shields her all day long,
and the one the Lord loves, rests between his shoulders.

He is wooing me from the jaws of distress
to a spacious place, free from restriction.
He rescued me, because he delighted in me.
You hear O Lord the desire of the afflicted;
You encourage them and you listen to their cry.
I called on your name, O Lord,
from the depths of the pit, you heard my plea:
"Do not close your ears to my cry for relief."
You came near when I called you,
and you said, "Do not fear,"
O Lord, you took up my case; you redeemed my life.
You have seen, O Lord, the wrong done to me.[27]

---

27 Paraphrased from Psalms 9:12; Job 36:15; Isaiah 63:9; Isaiah 40:11; Deuteronomy 33:12; Job 36:16; 2 Samuel 22:20; Psalms 10:17; and Lamentations 3:55–59.

CHAPTER Fifteen

ANXIETY AND FEAR

Search me, O God, and know my heart;
test me and know my anxious thoughts.
See if there is any
offensive [wounded] way in me,
and lead me in the way everlasting.
(Psalms 139:23–24)

AFTER MY RAGE AT MEN BEGAN TO SETTLE, I FOUND THAT IT WAS BEING replaced with intense anxiety whenever I was in a crowd. This feeling was comparable to someone telling you there's a spider on your collar about to go down your neck while you have your hands full and can't do anything about it.

From My Journal

There it is again, that uncomfortable feeling that settles in the pit of my stomach. It's not pain, really; it's more like an awareness that something isn't sitting right with me, an uneasiness that just won't go away, a restlessness of spirit that keeps me from feeling at peace with myself. It's a feeling that something terrible is about to happen. It's as though I've built my house on a sandbank and now I'm waiting, waiting, waiting for the rainy season to begin, to see if my house will stand against the storms of life.

Dear Jesus: I can't begin to express the heaviness in my soul that I feel right now. I don't know what to name it or where it is coming from. I don't know if it's anxiety or fear, but You know. And You know the slimy, dingy corner from which it slinks when I'm left alone with only myself for company. Father, show me the source from which this feeling seeps and bring it into Your light that we may examine it together. Please touch this aching area of my soul and give me Your peace.

[Grace,] cast all your anxiety on him because he cares for you. (1 Peter 5:7)

[He] has said, 'Never will I leave you [Grace]; never will I forsake you [Grace]... [therefore we] will not be afraid. (Hebrews.13:5–6)

Surely I am with you always [Grace], to the very end of the age. (Matthew 28:20)

[Grace,] let the peace of Christ rule in your heart... Let the word of Christ dwell in you richly. (Colossians 3:15–16)

For in the day of trouble he will keep [Grace] safe in his dwelling; he will hide [her] in the shelter of his tabernacle and set [her] high upon a rock. (Psalms 27:5)

I will praise the Lord, who counsels me... I have set the Lord always before me. Because he is at my right hand, I will not be shaken. Therefore my heart is glad... my body also will rest secure. (Psalms 16:7–9)

Fear had shadowed me for as long as I could remember. When my depression finally lifted, I developed a phobia. I couldn't go outside my house without someone with me. I couldn't handle crowds, so I wasn't able to attend church for over a year.

I asked my Heavenly Father to show me the roots of my fear, and through my healing process the source was traced back to before I was born, to when my mother was five months pregnant with me. While my older siblings were all at school, my four-year-old brother set our house on fire, then crawled under a bed to hide. As the house went up in flames around her, my mother, with an eighteen-month-old in her arms, searched the house for her other child. By the time she had rescued her children, she had burned her feet and the house was beyond saving.

As she stood trembling, watching her home disintegrate, her heart pounding wildly with the terror of nearly losing her children, fear took a stranglehold on the child within her body. Through counselling and my Heavenly Father's guidance, I relived the heat of the flames and the light of the fire that I experienced at that time through my mother's senses.

Fear showed itself again toward the end of my five-year healing journey. I decided to go back to school for retraining as a dental assistant, and on my way to the school to register I was in a subway car when it stopped in a tunnel. As I looked around, I realized that I was alone with a man sitting a couple of seats up from me. My heart started racing and my breathing became laboured. I think we were stopped there for no more than five minutes, but by the time the train started moving again I was soaked from head to toe from my own perspiration. I had spent the entire time praying for protection and talking myself down.

When I returned to work after my training, I found that the office I worked in had five people, which represented personalities of my childhood home, of which I still had unresolved issues. I found it very difficult to interact with these staff members because I was afraid of them.

One of the employers was very stern and businesslike, definitely a choleric temperament type. The other was easygoing and fun to work with. He was a phlegmatic and resembled my brother who had died five years previously. He even carried himself the same way. The receptionist was a mean-spirited woman, a choleric-melancholy whom I immediately feared. One employee took a dislike to me instantly and wouldn't talk to me, which also frightened me. The fifth person was nice to me, but I later found her to be deceitful, carrying gossip about me back to the rest of the staff. Other people coming and going represented other personalities of my childhood.

Having to interact with these people everyday caused many feeling flashbacks, resulting in childhood emotions coming to the surface. I would take a couple of minutes several times a day while I was in the darkroom developing x-rays to talk myself down from the panic that rose up and restricted my throat. I would take time to pray for protection and commit myself to my Good Shepherd to be carried in His arms.

One time, a male patient, about five years older than me, thought he was being funny by putting his arms around me when I leaned across him to adjust the x-ray machine. When he realized that I didn't get the joke, he said, "I was only teasing, I'm a married man." He may have been joking, but it was weeks before I was able to feel safe again. I wore a big lab coat over my one-size-too-large clothes to hide my shape. Somehow it seemed to give me a sense of security.

It was a very difficult time. Every day was filled with fear and anxiety, but I stuck it out until the Lord opened another door for me. Looking back, I see that my Heavenly Father had arranged this situation for me so that I would have to deal with old emotional wounds. It was a painful time, but also a healing time.

FEAR CAN MAKE YOU DO THE CRAZIEST THINGS

My husband and I made a point of getting away by ourselves for a weekend once or twice a year. On one occasion, we took a trip to Niagara Falls, Ontario. We arrived after dark on Friday night and made our way to the fifth floor of the hotel.

The following morning, my husband said, "I'm going to go out for a while and let you relax and have some time to yourself."

I chose to take this time to have a long, relaxing bubble bath. As the tub was filling up, I took my clothes off and walked around the hotel room. Since it had been dark the night before, I decided to take a peek out the window to see if I could see the falls. The window extended from floor to ceiling with a heavy drape covering it.

I very carefully pulled the window drape back so that only my face was visible in the window, taking every precaution not to let my naked body be seen. I noted that we were facing the front parking lot and didn't have much of a view. As I stood looking out the window, I suddenly heard a key in the door. Panicking, I jumped behind the window drape.

As it turned out, my husband had forgotten his wallet and had returned to the hotel room for it.

Now I know that some of my readers are rolling on the floor in a fit of laughter, but some of you are horrified that I would share such an intimate detail of my life. One of the things I have learned through my healing journey is to lighten up and not take myself so seriously. We need to learn to laugh at ourselves and the crazy things we do. *"A cheerful heart is good medicine"* (Proverbs 17:22). So go ahead and have a really good belly laugh at my expense.

God has said,
"Never will I leave you;
never will I forsake you,"
So we say with confidence,
"The Lord is my helper;
I will not be afraid."
(Hebrews 13:5-6)

DO NOT BE AFRAID

Do not fear,
do not let your hands hang limp.
The Lord your God is with you,
he is mighty to save.
Do not be afraid or discouraged
because of this vast army,
for the battle is not yours, but God's.
You will not have to fight this battle.
Take up your positions, stand firm
and see the deliverance the Lord will give you.
Do not be afraid;
do not be discouraged.
Go out to face them and the Lord will be with you.
Have faith in the Lord your God and you will be upheld.
God is our refuge and strength an ever-present help in trouble,
therefore we will not fear.
The Lord Almighty is with us,
the God of Jacob, [our God] is our fortress.

So do not fear, for I am with you.
Do not be dismayed, for I am your God.
I will strengthen you and help you;
I will uphold you with my righteous right hand.
For I am the Lord, your God,
who takes hold of your right hand and says to you,
"Do not fear; I will help you.
Do not be afraid,
for I myself, will help you," declares the Lord.

"Fear not, for I have redeemed you;
I have summoned you by name; you are mine.
When you pass through the waters, I will be with you:
and when you pass through the rivers,

they will not sweep over you.
When you walk through the fire,
you will not be burned;
the flames will not set you ablaze…
Since you, are precious and honoured in my sight,
…and because I love you
do not be afraid for I am with you.

…Do not be terrified;
do not be afraid,.
The Lord your God, who is going before you,
will fight for you…
the Lord your God carried you,
as a father carries his son,
all the way you went until you reached this place."

I sought the Lord, and he answered me;
he delivered me from all my fears.
When I am afraid, I will trust in you.
In God whose word I praise,
in God I trust; I will not be afraid.

Even though I walk through the valley
of the shadow of death,
I will fear no evil for you are with me.
I will lie down and sleep in peace,
for you alone, O Lord, make me dwell in safety.[28]

---

28 Paraphrased from Zephaniah 3:16; 2 Chronicles 20:15, 17, 20; Psalms 46:1–2, 7; Isaiah 41:10, 13–14; Isaiah 43:1–2 ,4–5; Deuteronomy 1:29–31; Psalms 34:4; Psalms 56:3–4; Psalms 23:4; and Psalms 4:8.

CHAPTER
Sixteen

Seeking the God Dependent Life

Lord, you establish peace for us;
all that we have accomplished
you have done for us.
(Isaiah 26:12)

DEPENDENCIES

When I was a young child and adolescent in school, I craved the attention of my teachers and other adults, lapping up all I could get from them. I fantasized about being special to them and being important in their lives. It was like my heart had a hole in it, and regardless of how much individuals showed me acceptance and appreciation, I just couldn't get filled up. Love-hunger ate away at my self-esteem constantly.

The young men I was attracted to in my teens were all products of dysfunctional homes, and it's nothing short of a miracle that I didn't end up married to an abusive husband.

At twenty-three years of age, after a short time of dating, I married a man who craved affection equally. Our wounded hearts cemented together into what appeared to be a very close marriage. In actuality, our relationship was an unhealthy codependent union. I was needy, and he needed to be needed.

Thirteen years later, I lost my father and my brother, on whom I was dependent, to cancer. Unable to accept the loss, I became emotionally unstable and developed other dependencies. Support groups helped me deal with this issue as I interacted with other people who struggled with dependencies.

As I became more aware of my body and state of mind, I began to see a pattern which set me up for failure in disciplining my mind. I was most vulnerable to dependencies when I was worried, anxious, afraid, or fatigued.

Worry, anxiety, and fear are direct indications that I'm not trusting God to meet my needs. As I had become accustomed to, I looked up scriptures on God's provision and memorized them so that I would have something to fight back with when these distractions came nagging at my mind.

So do not worry, saying, 'What shall we eat?' or 'What shall we drink?' or 'What shall we wear?'…your heavenly Father knows that you need them. But seek first his kingdom and his righteousness, and all these things will be given to you as well. (Matthew 6:31–33)

Which of you, if his son asks for bread, will give him a stone? Or if he asks for a fish, will give him a snake? If you, then… know how to give good gifts to your children, how much more will your Father in heaven give good gifts to those who ask him! (Matthew 7:9–11)

Consider the ravens: They do not sow or reap, they have no storeroom or barn; yet God feeds them. And how much more valuable you are than birds! Who of you by worrying can add a single hour to his life? Since you cannot do this very little thing, why do you worry about the rest? (Luke 12:24–26)

Cast all your anxiety on him because he cares for you. (1 Peter 5:7)

Do not be anxious about anything, but in everything, by prayer and petition with thanksgiving, present your requests to God. And the peace of God, which transcends all understanding, will guard your hearts and minds in Christ Jesus. (Philippians 4:6)

If God is for us, who can be against us? He who did not spare his own Son, but gave him up for us all—how will he not also, along with him, graciously give us all things? (Romans 8:31–32)

It's much easier to develop a dependency on someone or something which we can see than to learn to depend on God, whom we can't see. The things we depend on to calm our anxieties as an alternative to God are never satisfying for very long. They actually result in enslaving us.

My people have committed two sins: They have forsaken me, the spring of living water, and have dug their own cisterns, broken cisterns that cannot hold water. (Jeremiah 2:13)

Sow for yourselves righteousness, reap the fruit of unfailing love, and break up your unplowed ground; for it is time to seek the Lord, until he comes and showers righteousness on you. But you have planted wickedness, you have reaped evil, you have eaten the fruit of deception. Because you have depended on your own strength and on your many warriors [dependencies]. (Hosea 10:12–14)

Egypt will no longer be a source of confidence… but will be a reminder of… sin in turning to her for help. (Ezekiel 29:16)

CHOOSE WHOM YOU WILL SERVE

One day, as I was doing a Bible study on an unrelated topic, I stumbled onto a passage on the subject of dependencies. It hit me like a bolt of lightning.

This is what the Lord says: "Cursed is the one who trusts in man, who depends on flesh for his strength and whose heart turns away from the Lord. He will be like a bush in the wastelands; he will not see prosperity when it comes. He will dwell in the parched places of the desert, in a salt land where no one lives." (Jeremiah 17:5–6)

These verses tell me several things about myself and what my future holds, if I continue on the path that I'm on.

1. I cannot have God's blessing on my life if I look to my dependencies for strength and comfort.
2. If I look for acceptance and approval from people as an alternative to God, my heart will actually turn away from my Heavenly Father.
3. Leaning on dependencies to alleviate anxiety will result in my life being dry, barren, and fruitless.
4. I will never grow as a person or mature into a self-confident, resourceful individual.
5. I will become more and more isolated as others hurt me.

But blessed is the [woman] who trusts in the Lord, whose confidence is in him. [She] will be like a tree planted by the water that sends out its roots by the stream. It does not fear when heat comes; its leaves are always green. It has no worries in a year of drought and never fails to bear fruit. (Jeremiah 17:7–8)

These verses tell me what my life can be like if I walk away from my dependencies and became fully dependent on my Heavenly Father for all my needs—emotionally, physically, mentally, and spiritually.

1. I will be content if I trust my Heavenly Father to meet my needs.
2. I will grow as a person, be continually nourished, and fulfill my purpose.
3. I will not be constantly weighed down with worry, anxiety, and fear in everyday situations.
4. I will always be fresh and enthusiastic.

5. I will be confident that my physical needs will be met when finances are low.

6. I will be prosperous and bear fruit in my life. I will exemplify the fruit of the Spirit—love, joy, peace, patience, kindness, goodness, gentleness, faithfulness, and self-control.

My response to these verses was that of the prophet's:

Heal me, O Lord, and I will be healed; save me and I will be saved, for you are the one I praise. (Jeremiah 17:14)

MOVING BEYOND MY COMFORT ZONES

Learning to depend on God will mean moving out of my comfort zone. God has promised to be everything I need for every situation. The God-dependent life is to say, "When God is all I have left to hold on to, God will be enough."[29]

I read in Joshua 1:1–9 about the crisis Joshua faced at the time of Moses' death. The children of Israel had followed Moses for over forty years. Now Moses, their esteemed leader, was dead and Joshua was to take up the mantle and become the person in charge of this great mass of people. The group had become very comfortable living on the east side of the Jordan River. They—rather, their fathers—had rebelled before when told to enter the Promised Land.

How would this make Joshua feel? Was he afraid? Did he feel inadequate? Did he wonder if the multitude of people would accept him as their leader? Would they be willing to cross the Jordan River to take possession of the Promised Land?

Here's what God had to say to Joshua, and to us, when we become too complacent or dependent on people or our resources rather than on God, and are reluctant to move forward.

"After the death of Moses the servant of the Lord, the Lord said to Joshua son of Nun, Moses' aide: 'Moses my servant is dead'" (Joshua 1:1–2).

---

29 Author unknown.

Moses can no longer lead you because he is dead. You must let go of your dependency on your mentor and friend.

"Now then, you and all these people, get ready to cross the Jordan River into the land I am about to give to them—to the Israelites. I will give you every place where you set your foot, as I promised Moses" (Joshua 1:1–2).

Although you have become very comfortable with the situation as it is, you need to move out of your comfort zone so that I will be able to bless you as I have promised.

"No one will be able to stand up against you all of the days of your life" (Joshua 1:5).

I will be your strength, and you will have success in all that you set out to accomplish.

"As I was with Moses, so I will be with you" (Joshua 1:5).

God did not tell Joshua to be like Moses, but that He would be with him like He was with Moses, in his own unique style of leadership. I gave your friend and mentor all of his gifts, talents, and abilities and I will do the same for you.

"I will never leave you nor forsake you" (Joshua 1:5).

You do not need to depend on anyone to look after you. I am with you and I am all that you need in every situation, every day of your life. Trust Me. You can depend on Me.

"Be strong and courageous, because you will lead these people to inherit the land I swore to their forefathers to give them. Be strong and very courageous" (Joshua 1:6–7).

Change is not for cowards. It takes hard work and persistence. It takes courage to face all the dark shadows and move into unfamiliar territory. Courage is not the absence of fear, but the ability to press forward and conquer fear. If you will persevere, you will grow as a person and you will find an abundant life overflowing with hope and joy. In time, you will share your hope and healing journey with others.

126

"Be careful to obey all the law my servant Moses gave you; do not turn from it to the right or to the left... Do not let this Book of the Law depart from your mouth" (Joshua 1:7–8).

When you feel anxious, lonely or depressed, you are tempted to fill your emptiness with other dependencies and you may forget to draw your strength from Me. Stay close to Me, and I will help you.

"Meditate on it day and night, so that you may be careful to do everything written in it" (Joshua 1:8).

Spend time getting to know Me through reading your Bible. Pour out your heart to Me in your prayers and I will give you the scripture you need for comfort and strength. Memorize the ones that are most helpful and meditate on what each verse is saying to you. Pray them back to Me, out loud, in your own expression of thought. My words will be your guide through your healing journey.

"Then you will be prosperous and successful... wherever you go" (Joshua 1:9, 7).

The more time you spend with Me, the more My character will be developed in you and you will be successful. Continue your fellowship with Me and I will strengthen you as you move forward.

"Have I not commanded you? Be strong and courageous. Do not be terrified; do not be discouraged, for the Lord your God will be with you wherever you go" (Joshua 1:9).

Have I not commanded you to walk away from your comfort zone? If I have commanded you to do this, don't you think I will enable you to do it? Don't be afraid. Be strong and have courage, because I will be holding your hand all the way. It will be two or three steps forward, then one or two steps back, but do not be discouraged. This is the normal pattern of the healing journey. Just cling to Me. I will be with you and I will help you. I will strengthen you and uphold you. When you are too weary and weak to go on, I will carry you.

Listen to me...
you whom I have upheld since you were conceived,
and have carried since your birth.
Even to your old age and gray hairs I am he,
I am he who will sustain you.
I have made you and I will carry you;
I will sustain you and I will rescue you.
(Isaiah 46:3–4)

Do not be terrified; do not be afraid...
The Lord your God, who is going before you,
will fight for you...
the Lord your God carried you,
as a father carries his son,
all the way you went until you reached this place.
(Deuteronomy 1:29–31)

So do not throw away your confidence;
it will be richly rewarded.
You need to persevere
so that when you have done the will of God,
You will receive what he has promised.
(Hebrews 10:35–36)

CHAPTER

Seventeen

I AM ALL THAT YOU NEED

For your Father knows
what you need
before you ask him.
(Matthew 6:8)

I AM Your Comfort
As a [loving] mother comforts her child,
so will I comfort you; and you will be comforted...
(Isaiah 66:13)
He will call upon me,
and I will answer him;
I will be with him in trouble,
I will deliver him and honor him.
(Psalm 91:15)

I AM Your Confidence

For you have been my hope, O Sovereign Lord,
my confidence since my youth.
(Psalms 71:5)
You bestow glory on me and lift up my head.
(Psalms 3:3)
I can do everything through him who gives me strength.
(Philippians 4:13)
The fruit of righteousness will be peace;
The effect of righteousness
will be quietness and confidence forever.
(Isaiah 32:17)

I AM Your Counsellor

Pour out your hearts to him, for God is our refuge.
(Psalms 62:8)
I will counsel you and watch over you.
(Psalms 32:8)

I AM Your Foundation

He will be the sure foundation for your times,
a rich store of salvation and wisdom and knowledge;
the fear of the Lord is the key to this treasure.
(Isaiah 33:6)

I AM Your Guide

The Lord will guide you always; he will satisfy your needs
in a sun-scorched land and will strengthen your frame.
(Isaiah 58:11)

I AM Your Healer

"I will restore you to health and heal your wounds,"
declares the Lord.
(Jeremiah 30:17)

I AM Your Helper

So do not fear, for I am with you;
do not be dismayed, for I am your God.
I will strengthen you and help you;
I will uphold you with my righteous right hand.
(Isaiah 41:10)

I AM Your Hiding Place

You are my hiding place;
you will protect me from trouble
and surround me with songs of deliverance.
(Psalms 32:7)

I AM Your Hope

"For I know the plans I have for you," declares the Lord,
"plans to prosper you and not to harm you,
plans to give you hope and a future."
(Jeremiah 29:11)
May the God of hope fill you with all joy and peace
as you trust in him, so that you may overflow with hope
by the power of the Holy Spirit.
(Romans 15:13)
Christ in you the hope of glory.
(Colossians 1:27)

I AM Your Identity

You stoop down to make me great.
(Psalms 18:35)
...Love the Lord your God, listen to his voice,
and hold fast to him.
For the Lord is your life...
(Deuteronomy 30:20)

I AM Your Joy

[I will] go to the altar of God,

to God, my joy and my delight.
(Psalms 43:4)
You fill me with joy in your presence.
(Psalm 16:11)

I AM Your Light
You, O Lord, keep my lamp burning;
my God turns my darkness into light.
(Psalms 18:28)
For with you is the fountain of life;
in your light we see light.
(Psalm 36:9)

I AM the One who Loves You
I have loved you with an everlasting love;
I have drawn you with loving-kindness.
(Jeremiah 31:3)
He will take great delight in you,
he will quiet you with his love,
he will rejoice over you with singing.
(Zephaniah 3:17)
For God so loved the world
that he gave His one and only Son,
That whoever believes in him
shall not perish but have eternal life.
(John 3:16)
The Lord's unfailing love
surrounds the man who trusts in him.
(Psalm 32:10)

I AM Your Peace
The Lord gives strength to his people;
The Lord blesses his people with peace.
(Psalm 29:11)
A righteous man...

will have no fear of bad news;
his heart is steadfast, trusting in the Lord.
His heart is secure, he will have no fear.
(Psalm 112:6–8)
You will keep in perfect peace
him whose mind is steadfast,
Because he trusts in you.
(Isaiah 26:3)
He himself is our peace.
(Ephesians 2:13)

I AM Your Provider

The Lord is my shepherd, I shall not be in want.
(Psalms 23:1)
Put [your] hope in God,
who richly provides us with everything
for our enjoyment.
(1 Timothy 6:17)

I AM Your Refuge

The Lord is a refuge for the oppressed,
a stronghold in times of trouble.
(Psalms 9:9)
I will say of the Lord,
"He is my refuge and my fortress,
My God, in whom I trust."
He will cover you with his feathers,
And under his wings you will find refuge;
His faithfulness will be your shield and rampart.
(Psalm 91:2, 4)
How priceless is your unfailing love!
Both high and low among men find refuge
in the shadow of your wings.
(Psalm 36:7)

I AM Your Rest

Come to me, all you who are weary and burdened,
and I will give you rest.
(Matthew 11:28)
He who dwells in the shelter of the Most High
will rest in the shadow of the Almighty.
(Psalm 91:1)

I AM Your Rock

He lifted me out of the slimy pit, out of the mud and mire;
he set my feet on a rock and gave me a firm place to stand.
(Psalms 40:2)
The Lord is my rock, my fortress and my deliverer;
my God is my rock, in whom I take refuge.
(Psalms 18:2)

I AM Your Salvation

Salvation is found in no one else, for there is no other name
under heaven given to men by which we must be saved.
(Acts 4:12)
Believe in the Lord Jesus, and you will be saved...
(Acts 16:31)

I AM Your Shield

You are a shield around me, O Lord.
(Psalms 3:3)
He is my shield and the horn of my salvation ,my stronghold.
(Psalm 18:2)

I AM Your Strength

The Sovereign Lord is my strength;
he makes my feet like the feet of a deer,
he enables me to go on the heights.
(Habakkuk 3:19)
For the eyes of the Lord

range throughout the earth
to strengthen those whose hearts
are fully committed to him.
(2 Chronicles 16:9)
He gives strength to the weary
and increases the power of the weak.
(Isaiah 40:29)

I AM Your Teacher

I will instruct you and teach you in the way you should go.
(Psalms 32:8)
The Holy Spirit, whom the Father will send in my name,
will teach you all things.
(John 14:26)

I AM Your Truth

Jesus answered,
"I am the way and the truth and the life.
No one comes to the Father except through me."
(John 14:6)
Then you will know the truth,
and the truth will set you free.
(John 8:32)

I AM Your Wisdom

If any of you lacks wisdom, he should ask God,
who gives generously to all...
(James 1:5)

I AM All that You Need

And my God will meet all your needs
according to his glorious riches in Christ Jesus.
(Philippians 4:19)

CHAPTER

Eighteen

THOSE POWERFUL TEMPTATIONS

No temptation has seized you except what is common to man.
And God is faithful;
he will not let you be tempted beyond what you can bear.
But when you are tempted, he will also provide a way out
so that you can stand up under it.
(1 Corinthians 10:13)

THE BATTLE IN MY MIND

SATAN, BEING THE COWARD THAT HE IS, SEIZES THE MOMENT WHEN God's children are at their weakest to attack them. He watches for a time when they are overworked and exhausted, or have just experienced a great loss or victory, to fill their minds with lies and lead them into temptations. He takes full advantage of a crisis to pounce on his prey. Such was the case at the very beginning of my wilderness journey.

From My Journal

Satan Attacks. I feel like there is a war going on inside me. It's like a tug-of-war. Jesus is pulling me one way and Satan is pulling me the other. The temptation to give in to Satan is so strong that I can hardly stand it. Yet at the same time I feel the Holy Spirit drawing my heart to follow and obey the Lord I love. I feel like the apostle Paul, when he stated, *"I do not understand what I do. For what I want to do I do not do, but what I hate I do... For I have the desire to do what is good, but I cannot carry it out. For what I do is not the good I want to do; no, the evil I do not want to do—this I keep on doing"* (Romans 7:15, 18–19).

Over and over, Satan harassed me, filling my mind with lies and tempting me to destroy my life. Finally, after an hour of struggling, I dropped to my knees out of desperation and begged God to help me. Then Jesus whispered, *"Greater is he that is in you, than he that is in the world"* (1 John 4:4, KJV).

I read Psalms 139 and interacted with it in the margins of my Bible.

"O Lord, you have searched me and know me" (Psalms 139:1).
Lord, You know my emotional scars.

"You hem me in—behind and before; you have laid your hand on me" (Psalms 139:5).
I am Yours. My accuser can't harm me.

"Your hand will guide me, your right hand will hold me fast" (Psalms 139:10).
Lord, I am not holding on to You; You are holding on to me.

"All the days ordained for me were written in your book before one of them came to be" (Psalms 139:16).
Lord, You knew the harm that would be done to me even before I was born. You knew how it would mould my personality. You knew the weaknesses it would leave me with. You knew the temptations I would have to live with because of it.

"Search me, O God, and know my heart; test me and know my anxious thoughts" (Psalms 139:23).

Lord, know my emotional wounds, know my resulting weaknesses.

"See if there is any offensive way in me, and lead me in the way everlasting" (Psalms 139:24).

Lord, look at the emotional wounds I bear and lead me down Your path for my healing. Lord, I give You my emotions—broken, scarred, and crushed. I give You my fears, I give You my life.

> *[Grace], Satan has asked to sift you as wheat.*
> *But I have prayed for you, [Grace] that your faith may not fail.*
> *And when you have turned back, strengthen your brothers.*
> (Luke 22:31–32)

> *But the Lord stood by my side and gave me strength*
> *so that through me the message might be fully proclaimed...*
> *And I was delivered from the lion's mouth.*
> *The Lord will rescue me from every evil attack*
> *and will bring me safely to his heavenly kingdom.*
> *To him be glory for ever and ever. Amen.*
> (2 Timothy 4:17–18)

From My Journal

Walking the Tightrope. I feel like I'm walking on a tightrope, blindfolded. I'm tipping back and forth, waiting to fall. On one side is the temptation to turn my back on God and run away from everything I believe and love, to follow a path of self-destruction. On the other side is suicide. Which side will I fall off? Any day now, I'm going to fall. I can't go on. I can't take any more of this tipping back and forth. Lord, don't let me fall!

Dear Jesus, I'm too weak to go on. I can't fight this emotional war anymore. Good Shepherd, please just lift me into Your arms and carry me like a wounded sheep. Please don't let me fall. Don't let Satan win this battle.

My Heavenly Father answered me with His Word.

He tends His flock like a shepherd: He gathers the lambs in his arms and carries them close to his heart; he gently leads those that have young. (Isaiah. 40:11)

The eternal God is your refuge, and underneath are the everlasting arms. (Deuteronomy 33:27)

Lord, You never tire of carrying me.

I said, "You are my servant"; I have chosen you and have not rejected you. So do not fear, for I am with you; do not be dismayed, for I am your God. I will strengthen you and help you; I will uphold you with my righteous right hand... For I am the Lord, your God, who takes hold of your right hand and says to you, Do not fear; I will help you. Do not be afraid... for I myself will help you. (Isaiah 41:9–10, 13–14)

From My Journal

Dear Jesus, thank you that Your hand is under me waiting to catch me if I fall. You know my heart. You know I love You and long to serve You. Thank you that I can rest in Your arms. Someday I will thank You for leading me through this wilderness journey. Someday I will be strong enough to walk beside You again. Someday I will use this experience to help someone else. But for now, just let me rest in You.

Unless the Lord had given me help, I would soon have dwelt in the silence of death. When I said, 'My foot is slipping,' your love, O Lord, supported me. When anxiety was great within me, your consolation brought joy to my soul. (Psalms 94:17–19)

If the Lord delights in a man's way, he makes his steps firm; though he stumble, he will not fall, for the Lord upholds him with his hand. (Psalms 37:23–24)

Temptation starts in the mind. You can look at something you desire and quickly look away before temptation is able to rear its ugly head. It's when you entertain the thought that Satan gains a foothold in your mind. If you do this often enough, it becomes a habit. Suddenly you realize that you no longer have the control to walk away from that nagging temptation. You're trapped in Satan's snare. *"Sin is crouching at your door; it desires to have you, but you must master it"* (Genesis 4:7).

Thus begins the long tedious battle in your mind, swimming upstream against the current to regain lost ground. You swim frantically for awhile and make progress, but then you tire and the current carries you back to where you began. You try again and again and again and again, but each time you become exhausted and end up being carried back to where you started. You're weighed down with guilt, fear, and depression. You are in bondage.

The only way to be released is to acknowledge your helplessness to yourself, and to your Heavenly Father, and ask for His help. Then, with the help of your Heavenly Father, you fight with every ounce of energy you possess and then rely on His strength to get you over the top. You will fail many, many times before you gradually begin to see progress.

My eyes are ever on the Lord,
for only he will release my feet from the snare.
(Psalms 25:15)

I can do everything through him
who gives me strength.
(Philippians 4:13)

CHAPTER

Nineteen

Bondage

A man is a slave
to whatever has mastered him.
(2 Peter 2:19)

During an extended crisis, escape techniques that have been our comfort for years become more habitual. Pesky little temptations that have plagued a person for a lifetime unexpectedly become persistent. Persistent temptations become obsessions, and before you know it obsessions become bondage.

THE BONDAGE CYCLE

We tend to go around the bondage cycle in a pattern, each developing our own style. We go around it so often that we dig a rut that keeps us habitually going around and around and around. Everything seems to be going well; our fellowship with our Heavenly Father is good. Then stress enters our lives, be it worry, fatigue, illness or some other form of anxiety, and the cycle begins.

Stress → Escape Techniques → Resisting Temptation → Submitting to Temptation → Guilt → Fear → Depression → Repentance → Joy → Peace → Prayer → Stress → Escape Techniques →Resisting Temptation → Submitting to Temptation → Guilt → Fear → Depression → Repentance → Joy → Peace → Prayer → Stress →
Around and around we go.

Stress: Worry, fatigue, illness, and anxiety.
We are hard pressed on every side. (2 Corinthians 4:8)

In this world you will have trouble. (John 16:33)

Escape Techniques: Shopping, eating, fiction, TV, gambling, alcohol, drug abuse, fantasizing, pornography, or compulsive behaviours of any kind.
…you have eaten the fruit of deception. Because you have depended on your own strength. (Hosea 10:13)

How is it that you are turning back to those weak and miserable principles [ways of coping]? Do you wish to be enslaved by them all over again? (Galatians 4:9)

Are you so foolish? After beginning with the Spirit, are you now trying to attain your goal by human effort? Have you suffered so much for nothing…? (Galatians 3:3–4)

Resisting Temptation: Have a game plan.
Prepare your minds for action; be self-controlled. (1 Peter 1:13)

Be self-controlled and alert. Your enemy the devil prowls around like a roaring lion looking for someone to devour. (1 Peter 5:8)

We take captive every thought and make it obedient to Christ. (2 Corinthians 10:5)

Fix your thoughts on Jesus. (Hebrews 3:1)

Submit yourselves, then, to God. Resist the devil, and he will flee from you. (James 4:7)

Submitting to Temptation: Losing the battle.

Everyone who sins is a slave to sin. (John 8:34)

For a man is a slave to whatever has mastered him. (2 Peter 2:19)

Don't you know that when you offer yourselves to someone to obey him as slaves, you are slaves to the one whom you obey...? (Romans 6:16)

Guilt: The Holy Spirit convicts for the purpose of repentance.

When I kept silent, my bones wasted away through my groaning all day long. For day and night your hand was heavy upon me; my strength was sapped as in the heat of summer. (Psalms 32:3–4)

For I know my transgressions, and my sin is always before me. (Psalms 51:3)

My bones have no soundness because of my sin. My guilt has overwhelmed me like a burden too heavy to bear. (Psalms 38:3–4)

Fear: Our tempter becomes our accuser, saying, "God will never forgive."

Lord, do not rebuke me in your anger or discipline me in your wrath. For your arrows have pierced me... (Psalms 38:1–2)

Do not withhold your mercy from me, O Lord... For troubles without number surround me; my sins have overtaken me, and I cannot see. (Psalms 40:11–12)

Do not hide your face from me, do not turn your servant away in anger. (Psalms 27:9)

Depression: Hopelessness.

Hope deferred makes the heart sick... (Proverbs 13:12)

The evil deeds of a wicked man ensnare him; the cords of his sin hold him fast. (Proverbs 5:22)

My wounds fester and are loathsome because of my sinful folly. I am bowed down and brought very low; all day long I go about mourning... I am feeble and utterly crushed; I groan in anguish of heart. (Psalms 38:5–6, 8)

I have become as broken pottery. (Psalms 31:12)

What a wretched man I am! Who will rescue me from this body of death? (Romans 7:24)

Repentance: Ask for forgiveness.

If we confess our sins, he is faithful and just and will forgive us our sins and purify us from all unrighteousness. (1 John 1:9)

Create in me a pure heart, O God, and renew a steadfast spirit within me. (Psalms 51:10)

Then I acknowledged my sin to you and did not cover up my iniquity, I said, "I will confess my transgressions to the Lord"—and you forgave the guilt of my sin. (Psalms 32:5)

So if the Son sets you free, you will be free indeed. (John 8:36)

Though we are slaves, our God has not deserted us in our bondage. He has shown us kindness... He has granted us new life to rebuild [our souls] the house of our God and repair its ruins, and he has given us a wall of protection... (Ezra 9:9)

Joy: The absence of sin and guilt results in worship.

Restore to me the joy of your salvation and grant me a willing spirit, to sustain me. (Psalms 51:12)

Light is shed upon the righteous and joy on the upright in heart. (Psalms 97:11)

You have made known to me the path of life; you will fill me with joy in your presence, with eternal pleasures at your right hand. (Psalms 16:11)

You turned my wailing into dancing; you removed my sackcloth and clothed me with joy. (Psalms 30:11)

Peace: Trust in our Heavenly Father.

You will go out with joy and be led forth in peace. (Isaiah 55:12)

The Lord gives strength to his people; the Lord blesses his people with peace. (Psalms 29:11)

You will keep in perfect peace him whose mind is steadfast, because he trusts in you. (Isaiah 26:3)

The effect of righteousness will be quietness and confidence forever. (Isaiah 32:17)

Prayer: Communion with our Heavenly Father.

I cry aloud to the Lord; I lift up my voice to the Lord for mercy. I pour out my complaint before him; before him I tell my trouble. When my spirit grows faint within me, it is you who know my way. (Psalms 142:1–3)

Trust in him at all times, O people; pour out your hearts to him, for God is our refuge. (Psalms 62:8)

In my day of trouble I will call to you, for you will answer me. (Psalms 86:7)

The good news is we don't need to keep going around and around the bondage cycle. We can choose to go directly to prayer when stressed or anxious and pour out all our emotions to our Heavenly Father. If we take the time to tell God exactly what is happening in our lives and how we feel about it, the stress will be released and the need to turn to our obsessions will be diminished.

If we find that we're already several steps into the bondage cycle, we can take a shortcut to repentance, then pour out our heart to our Father. Our joy, peace, and fellowship will be restored. With practice, much practice, the bondage cycle will be reduced to a few steps with quick repentance. The key is to catch yourself as soon as your mind begins to wander toward your obsession. *"We take captive every thought and make it obedient to Christ"* (2 Corinthians 10:5). Then replace that thought with something glorifying to God, be it prayer, worship songs, or memorized Scripture. *"Fix your thoughts on Jesus"* (Hebrews 3:1).

As a means to fight temptation, I looked up every scripture I could find on my particular concern and began memorizing them. Following Jesus' example, I began quoting Scripture, out loud, when I was being tempted. I played praise music while I was going to sleep at night to keep my mind from wandering to areas that it shouldn't.

Another means that helped me overcome my obsessions was to keep my mind busy doing something productive:

- Doing something kind for someone else.
- Investing in other people's lives.
- Sharing what I was learning with other survivors.
- Helping those less fortunate than myself.

Trust in the Lord and do good... (Psalms 37:3)

MY HEAVENLY FATHER REAFFIRMS HIS LOVE

In my slow, snail-like progress, many times I became frustrated with myself. I continually cried out to my Heavenly Father for help and healing. I wondered if He was getting annoyed with me. Then I found some wonderful verses in Hosea and Isaiah that demonstrated God's love and patience with His people.

> *"She decked herself with rings and jewelry, and went after her lovers, but me she forgot," declares the Lord. "Therefore I am now going to allure her; I will lead her into the desert and speak tenderly to her. There I will give her back her vineyards, and will make the Valley of Achor [Valley of Trouble] a door of hope. There she will sing as in the days of her youth."* (Hosea 2:13–15)

> *I will heal their waywardness and love them freely.* (Hosea 14:4)

> *The Valley of Achor [Valley of Trouble] [will become] a resting place... for my people who seek me.* (Isaiah 65:10)

I took these little gems, personalized them, and applied them to my heart.

God said:

> Grace pursued comfort, love, and her own means of escape from her anxiety instead of coming to Me. She didn't trust Me

149

enough to help her through the hard times. Therefore, I am going to cause her to be caught up in her sin. I will lead Grace into the desert of a painful healing experience, through the valley of loneliness, depression, and fear.

There I will speak tenderly to her; I will comfort her with My Word and surround her with My love. When she is suffering, she will be ready to listen to My voice. I will calm her and demonstrate My love to her.

There in that place of pain, I will cause Grace to produce new fruit in her life. I will widen her experience and broaden her ministry. I will make her valley of trouble a door of hope. Through her agonizing experience, Grace will receive new life, new hope, and new dreams. Her walk and her fellowship with Me will be rejuvenated.

From now on, Grace will walk closely by My side and she will enjoy sweet fellowship with Me. Her valleys of trouble will become a place where she will learn to rest in Me throughout all the seasons of her life.

I have loved you with an everlasting love; I have drawn you with loving-kindness. (Jeremiah 31:3)

"Everlasting love" means that it goes on forever. It never stops from the day we are conceived to eternity. God cannot stop loving His children because to stop loving would be for God to deny His own character. *"God is love"* (1 John 4:16). Love is what God is.

> *The Lord your God is with you [Grace], he is mighty to save.*
> *He will take great delight in you [Grace],*
> *he will quiet you with his love,*
> *he will rejoice over you [Grace] with singing.*
> *The sorrows for the appointed feasts I will remove from you;*
> *They are a burden and a reproach to you [Grace].*
> (Zephaniah 3:17–18)

*"Do not be terrified; [Grace,] do not be afraid...
The Lord your God, who is going before you,
will fight for you [Grace], as he did... in the desert...
The Lord your God carried you [Grace],
as a father carries his son,
all the way you went until you reached this place."*
(Deuteronomy 1:29–31)

*Surely it was for my benefit that I suffered such anguish.
In your love you kept me from the pit of destruction;
you have put all my sins behind your back.*
(Isaiah 38:17)

FIGHTING THE BATTLE

This is a people plundered and looted,
all of them trapped in pits or hidden away in prisons.
They have become plunder, with no one to rescue them.
The eyes of the Lord range throughout the earth
to strengthen those whose hearts are fully committed to him.
Lord, there is no one like you to help the powerless against the mighty.
Help us, O Lord our God, for we rely on you.

He reached down from on high and took hold of me;
he drew me out of deep waters.
He rescued me from my powerful enemy,
from my foes, who were too strong for me.
…The Lord was my support.
He brought me out into a spacious place;
he rescued me because he delighted in me.

You are my lamp, O Lord;
the Lord turns my darkness into light.
With your help I can advance against a troop;
with my God I can scale a wall.

It is God who arms me with strength
and makes my way perfect.
He trains my hands for battle…
You give me your shield of victory;
you stoop down to make me great.
You broaden the path beneath me,
so that my ankles do not turn.
You armed me with strength for battle.

Be strong and courageous.
Do not be afraid or discouraged…
for there is a greater power with us than with him.
With him is only the arm of flesh,
but with us is the Lord our God to help us
and to fight our battles.
Be strong and courageous, and do the work.
Do not be afraid or discouraged,
for the Lord God, my God, is with you.
He will not fail you or forsake you
until all the work
for the service of [my soul]
the temple of the Lord is finished.

The Lord is with you when you are with him.
If you seek him, he will be found by you…
Be strong and do not give up,
for your work will be rewarded.
He holds victory in store for the upright,
he is a shield to those whose walk is blameless,
for he guards the course of the just
and protects the way of his faithful ones.[30]

---

30 Paraphrased from Isaiah 42:22; 2 Chronicles 16:9; 2 Chronicles 14:11; 2 Samuel 22:17–20, 29–30, 33, 35–37,40; 2 Chronicles 32:7–8; 1 Chronicles 28:20; 2 Chronicles 15:2, 7; and Proverbs 2:7–8.

PART
Three

THE REDEMPTIVE JOURNEY

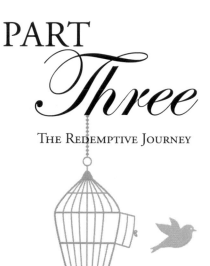

*They will rebuild the ancient ruins
and restore the [inner] places long devastated;
they will renew the ruined [relationships]
that have been devastated for generations.*
(Isaiah 61:4)

CHAPTER

Twenty

FORGIVENESS

"In your anger do not sin":
Do not let the sun go down
while you are still angry,
and do not give the devil a foothold.
(Ephesians 4:26-27)

THE HIGH COST OF FORGIVENESS

FORGIVENESS IS ANOTHER MAJOR AND NECESSARY STEP TOWARD healing. Forgiveness sets me free to move through the healing process and continue to grow as a person. Yet I have the liberty to choose to be either bitter or better. When I don't choose to forgive, all my other relationships will be contaminated by bitterness, and I will inevitably hurt those I love most. Refusing to forgive leaves an individual open to Satan's attacks and temptations. Frankly, Satan comes knocking on my door often enough without my leaving the porch light on for him. When I choose to be better, I am opening the door to allow God to change me as an individual.

Forgiving my offender means giving up my right to demand retribution. By forgiving the one who hurt me, I'm not saying that what he did was okay. Nor am I saying that I'm over the emotional pain. Forgiveness simply means that I am willing to live with the consequences of his sin against me. I let him off my hook, but he is still answerable to God.

Forgiveness is an unending growing experience in which we never seem to arrive. Just when we think we have the course of action down pat, we get thrown another curve and we have to start working through the process again.

David Augsburger has written a wonderful little book on forgiveness, entitled *The Freedom of Forgiveness*, which I have found very helpful. In it, he stresses:

> No matter how often we have forgiven or have been forgiven by others, we are all still learning to forgive. Forgiveness is not a skill that is mastered and becomes second nature. It must be faced each time injury or injustice strikes.
> Forgiveness is not a gift one claims, internalizes, and then possesses for life. It must be rediscovered in each situation of pain. We never grow beyond the learning stage. We never go beyond the level of student.[31]

> Forgiveness is difficult because it is very costly. The cost may require us to risk further hurt by exploring the injured relationship with someone who caused the injury to begin with. The cost may be that we will have to absorb pain without any satisfactory release and restoration. The cost may require us to accept further rejection when the other brushes us off, blames us further, burns us with additional anger, or blatantly refuses to talk.[32]

---

31 Augsburger, David. *The Freedom of Forgiveness* (Chicago, IL: Moody Publishers, 1988), pp. 41–42.
32 Ibid. p. 48.

Forgiveness, although very painful, is a vital ingredient to healing and is much preferred to the alternative. It has been said that "to refuse to forgive and choose to nurture bitterness toward my offender is like drinking poison and waiting for the other person to die."[33] According to *The Freedom of Forgiveness*, "Central to the work of forgiveness is the task of working through our feelings of anger."[34]

Forgiveness is a process. When we have been wounded deeply, we are unable to forgive instantly. We tend to need to move through several phases of forgiveness, linking various emotions, before we reach the desired end result of reconciliation.

Forgiving someone who has hurt us is hard work. It doesn't come naturally. In fact, everything in our being shouts, "FIGHT BACK! GET EVEN! RETALIATE!" We say, "He must pay for the pain he has caused me" or "Pain must be paid for."

But God says,

Do not repay anyone evil for evil. Be careful to do what is right in the eyes of everybody. If it is possible, as far as it depends on you, live at peace with everyone. Do not take revenge, my friends, but leave room for God's wrath, for it is written: "It is mine to avenge; I will repay," says the Lord. (Romans 12:17–19)

Yes, someone must pay. Yes, pain must be paid for, and someone has paid. Someone has paid for my pain with His very life. His name is Jesus.

One Sunday morning, during the communion service, the Lord showed me that where there are wounded people, there are those who have caused the hurt. And where there is healing for the victim, there is also healing for the perpetrator. He reminded me of Psalms 107:20: *"He sent his word, and healed them, and delivered them from their destructions"* (KJV).

The Holy Spirit then guided me through Isaiah 53:3–5.

---

33 Author unknown.

34 Augsburger, David. *The Freedom of Forgiveness* (Chicago, IL: Moody Publishers, 1988), p. 52.

He was… a man of sorrows, and familiar with suffering… Surely he took up my infirmities [my wounds, my weaknesses] and carried my sorrows [He feels the feeling of my emotional pain]… the punishment that brought [me] peace [from my sin and emotional pain] was upon him, and by his wounds [I] am healed.

The blood of Jesus Christ wasn't shed only to save me from my sins. It was also shed to heal me of the sins others have sinned against me, causing my emotional wounds. Those deep emotional wounds, inflicted upon me at the hands of selfish individuals, were being healed by the blood of Jesus Christ.

The blood of Jesus, his Son, purifies us from ALL sin [both my sins and the sins of others against me]. (1 John 1:7, emphasis added)

He also showed me that His blood was shed so that my abusers could be forgiven and healed of their destructions. There is healing, whether you are a victim or a perpetrator.

A BIBLICAL EXAMPLE OF FORGIVENESS

Joseph was seventeen when he was sold by his brothers as a slave (Genesis 37:2–11). His brothers hated him because he was his father's favourite son and had been given the richly ornamented robe of a prince. When Joseph had two dreams about his brothers bowing down to him, they hated him even more. Possibly they were afraid Joseph's dreams would come true and that their father would give him the birthright, making him the next patriarch and leader of the family. If that were the case, they would end up serving Joseph.

"Here comes that dreamer!" they said to each other. "Come now, let's kill him and throw him into one of these cisterns… then we'll see what comes of his dreams." (Genesis 37:19–20)

Reuben tried to rescue him and suggested throwing him into a cistern which had no water in it.

> *So when Joseph came to his brothers, they stripped him of his robe—the richly ornamented robe he was wearing—and they took him and threw him into the cistern."* (Genesis 37:23–24)

But when a caravan of Ishmaelites came by on their way to Egypt, the brothers sold Joseph to them as a slave.

Thirteen years later: *"Joseph was thirty years old when he entered the service of Pharaoh king of Egypt"* (Genesis 41:46). Then there were seven years of abundant crops followed by two years of famine before Joseph saw his brothers again (Genesis 41:29; 45:6). So a total of twenty-two years after Joseph had his dreams, they were fulfilled, when the brothers unknowingly bowed down to Joseph, who was the next in command to Pharaoh.

Joseph recognized his brothers but did not reveal his identity until he had tested them to see if they had changed. When he did disclose his identity, he said, *"I am your brother Joseph, the one you sold into Egypt!"* (Genesis 45:4) In his forgiveness of them, Joseph didn't downplay what they had done to him. He didn't say, "It's okay, guys. I know you didn't mean it." He didn't pretend it didn't happen. He called it for what it was. They had done a terrible thing to him and Joseph did not cover it up. It was clear to all concerned what had taken place. He gave them an opportunity to ask for forgiveness, so that their relationship could be restored.

After their father's death, the brothers were afraid that Joseph would retaliate. *"But Joseph said to them... 'Am I in the place of God?'"*(Genesis 50:19), acknowledging that vengeance belongs to the Lord.

> *"You intended to harm me, but God intended it for good [You couldn't have touched me if God hadn't allowed it] but God intended it for good to accomplish what is now being done, the saving of many lives. So then, don't be afraid. I will provide for you and your children." And he reassured them and spoke kindly to them.* (Genesis 50:20–21)

Joseph demonstrated his forgiveness of his brothers by the gentleness with which he treated them.

Therefore, as God's chosen people,
holy and dearly loved,
clothe yourselves with compassion,
kindness, humility, gentleness, and patience.
Bear with each other
and forgive whatever grievances
you may have against one another.
Forgive [the same way] as the Lord forgave you.
(Colossians 3:12-13)

CHAPTER
Twenty-one

THE PROCESS OF FORGIVENESS

Be kind and compassionate
to one another,
forgiving each other,
just as in Christ God forgave you."
(Ephesians 4:32)

FORGIVENESS DOESN'T COME EASILY WHEN YOU HAVE BEEN HURT DEEPLY. It will take many attempts, involving the whole gamut of emotions.

1. Forgiveness, as an act of the will. I forgave as an act of my will. Forgiveness isn't an emotion; it's an act of my will, so I can choose to forgive even though I don't feel like it. I can forgive with the grace God gives me. Scripture says I must forgive:

> *For if you forgive men when they sin against you, your heavenly*
> *Father will also forgive you. But if you do not forgive men their*
> *sins, your Father will not forgive your sins.* (Matthew 6:14–15)

I definitely wanted my sins to be forgiven, so I had little choice in whether or not I would forgive.

Later in my healing process, I learned the significance of why God wouldn't forgive me if I didn't forgive others. If I decide not to forgive those who have hurt me, then God cannot forgive me, because the same blood that cleanses me from my sin also cleanses those who have sinned against me.

The blood of Jesus, his Son, purifies us from ALL sin. (1 John 1:7, emphasis added)

Without the shedding of blood there is NO forgiveness. (Hebrews 9:22, emphasis added)

God says that Jesus, His Son, has already paid the debt in full. To say that the precious blood of Christ isn't sufficient to pay for another person's sin against me is an insult to the death of Jesus Christ. It is because God has forgiven me that I am able to forgive others their sins against me.

2. Forgiveness, to set myself free. In the initial phase of my forgiving process, I forgave since that was what I needed to do to set myself free from my offenders and perpetrators. If I don't forgive, I am held in bondage to the one I have not forgiven.

While walking my little Bichon Frise, Evian, I began to think about the control I had over her with her retractable leash. When I choose to, I can let the leash out full length and let her take her time walking, wandering, and sniffing, trying to find the perfect location to leave her little deposit. Although she appears to have her freedom, she can go no farther than the end of her leash.

When another dog comes along, I shorten the leash somewhat to prevent her from getting tangled in the other dog's leash while they say their hellos and do their routine sniffing of each other. Sometimes Evian takes a disliking to the other dog and gets a little nippy, so I draw her leash in shorter to have better control over her. However, she often pulls on the leash and we engage in a tug-of-war.

When we meet a large dog, Evian goes on the defensive and tries to take the other dog out before she has a chance to get hurt. Although Evian weighs only fifteen pounds, she has no problem letting a one hundred pound German shepherd know who's boss. What she lacks in size she makes up for in noise.

As I thought about the control I have over Evian while using the leash, I began to think about the control I let people have over me when I refuse to forgive them. It's like I willingly let them put a leash around my neck and keep me on a string like a yo-yo, as they bounce me up and down at their bidding. Even when they appear to leave me alone and let me have my freedom, I'm always waiting for the next incident. If they have a bad day, they can shorten my leash and get right in my face, jerking me around to suit their own emotional needs and agendas.

On the other hand, I can become the aggressor and go on the defensive, watching for every opportunity to overpower and control the one I have on the other end of the leash. Although it can be as comical as watching Evian go after a dog six times her own size, a woman harassing a man over two hundred and fifty pounds is likewise futile. A small person with a loud voice and abusive words can be very intimidating sometimes, even to a much larger person, yet how happy is she? The people on both ends of the leash are miserable.

Constantly waiting for the next episode of confrontation causes continuous anxiety, an incessant churning of the stomach that eats away at your soul. Anger, rage, bitterness, hatred, and vengeance strangle the life out of a person and rob her of the joy of her salvation. They are toxins that destroy the spirit. But there is hope! I can decide to set myself free from my adversary by cutting the leash. I can simply choose to forgive.

3. Forgiveness, by gaining understanding. As I healed, I learned to forgive by gaining an understanding of the wounds of the person who hurt me. Where are they coming from? How were they hurt in the past? Why might they have hurt me? Although none of the answers to these questions condones the behaviour of the other person, having an understanding of the person's background helps me have compassion for them and I, by the grace of God, am able to forgive.

4. Forgiveness, out of gratitude. As I grew in my relationship with the Lord, I learned to forgive, because Christ had paid the ultimate price so that God could forgive me. I forgave out of gratitude and love for God. Not forgiving would be sinful and I didn't want anything to disconnect me from fellowship with my Heavenly Father.

5. Forgiveness, to meet a need. Later, I got to the place where I forgave because that was what my offender needed. My lack of forgiveness may keep him from asking for God's forgiveness, thus preventing him from having a right relationship with God. My unforgiving heart might also prevent him from forgiving himself, which would affect the way he feels about himself.

6. Forgiveness, for reconciliation. Finally, I forgave for the purpose of experiencing reconciliation with those who have hurt me. Although reconciliation is the ultimate goal, it is not always attainable. One party may no longer be living, or the other party may refuse to meet and discuss the issues. He either ignores your request or he insists that nothing happened. In a case where there was violence involved, it may be dangerous for the survivor to re-establish the relationship with the former abuser. But we can still choose to forgive and release the offender into the hands of our Heavenly Father. My refusal to forgive would prevent reconciliation and consequently destroy any possible future relationship of any depth.

David Augsburger's book states,

> Before real forgiveness could take place, the two would need to remember the pain together, recall the injury together, recognize real repentance together, and agree to forget together.[35]

Such was the case of one of my offenders. With tears streaming down his face, he acknowledged the sin he had inflicted on me and asked me to forgive him. At this point, I acknowledged my forgiveness of him and so started the rebuilding of our new relationship together.

This situation took place at the beginning of my healing process. Although I had forgiven him for hurting me, I still had to deal with

35 Ibid., pp. 44–45.

the consequences of his sin in my life. Forgiveness doesn't wipe out the aftereffects of some wounds, but it does release you to receive the Lord's healing in your life as you work toward wholeness.

My relationships have been restored. Each and every offender is forgiven and we have moved on.

God, in His great mercy, gave me other blessings also. For the last few years of his life, my father became a different man. He fell in love with the Lord and studied his Bible daily. Whenever he had the opportunity, he loved to discuss the new insights God was giving him. I had many wonderful such talks with my father those last few years before the Lord took him home. He was a forgiven man. I loved my father dearly and was at his bedside when he slipped into eternity.

BIBLICAL STEPS FOR RESTORING RELATIONSHIPS

- **Ask yourself, "Why am I angry?"** *"In your anger do not sin... search your hearts and be silent"* (Psalms 4:4). Am I being oversensitive? Why am I reacting in this way? Is this anger a flashback to a previous wound? Ask God to show you what the true source of your pain is.

- **Ask yourself, "Where am I guilty of the same offense?"** *"First take the plank out of your own eye, and then you will see clearly to remove the speck from your brother's eye"* (Matthew 7:5). Ask God to show you your blind spots.

- **Go to your offender.** *"If your brother sins against you, go and show him his fault, just between the two of you. If he listens to you, you have won your brother over. But if he will not listen, take one or two others along, so that 'every matter may be established by the testimony of two or three witnesses'"* (Matthew 18:15). If someone has hurt me, I am to go to him quietly and tell him what he has done or said that has hurt me. I am to tell him *one fault*; I am not to back my truck up and dump a lifetime of offenses on his front lawn. Nor am I supposed to run around talking to everyone else about the situation first. I am to go to him quietly, in a gentle manner, not in an accusatory attitude, and express my concerns. If he listens to me, the relationship can be restored without anyone knowing about the details. If he won't discuss the issue, I am to take one or two other trustworthy people with me as witnesses or as mediators.

- **Listen attentively.** *"Everyone should be quick to listen, slow to speak and slow to become angry"* (James 1:19–20). Misunderstandings happen when we start talking before we have understood what the other person has said. We need to give them a chance to explain what they mean. We need to listen for what they are not saying; we need to understand their feelings.

- **Respond gently.** *"A gentle answer turns away wrath, but a harsh word stirs up anger"* (Proverbs 15:1). Respond to accusations with a gentle answer. Keep your voice calm. Use words like, "I hear you saying..." or "Do I understand you correctly?" Use the words "I feel" rather than "you are" or "you did."

- **Don't judge.** *"Be completely humble and gentle; be patient, bearing with one another in love"* (Ephesians 4:2). We all make mistakes, so keep in mind that you may be in his shoes tomorrow.

- **Say only what is helpful to the listener.** *"Do not let any unwholesome talk come out of your mouths, but only what is helpful for building others up according to their needs, that it may benefit those who listen... Get rid of all bitterness, rage and anger, brawling and slander, along with every form of malice. Be kind and compassionate to one another, forgiving each other, just as in Christ God forgave you"* (Ephesians 4:29, 31–32). Don't use your words to beat up your offender or dump your feelings, making yourself feel that you have been heard. Use only what is helpful to the listener. What does the listener need to hear so that he can understand your point?

- **Control your anger.** *"'In your anger do not sin': Do not let the sun go down while you are still angry, and do not give the devil a foothold"* (Ephesians 4:26–27). Anger in itself is not a sin; it is an emotion. It's what we do with our anger that can be sinful. Do we harbour it? Nurture it? Do we let it fester until it becomes bitterness? Don't let the sun go down while you're still angry. Deal with the situation quickly before Satan has a chance to ensnare you with it. If you can't resolve the issue, agree to disagree for the time being and set a time to meet again to resolve any unsettled issues.

- **Ask forgiveness for your offences.** *"If you are offering your gift at the altar and there remember that your brother has something against you, leave your gift there in front of the altar. First go and be reconciled to your brother; then come and offer your gift"* (Matthew 5:23–24). Often when someone hurts us, we automatically say or do something hurtful in return. Never mind what she did to me, I am to ask forgiveness of those whom I have hurt, before I offer my praise and worship to God. How can I worship when I am in conflict with someone?

FORGIVENESS FOR MYSELF

Wounded people wound other people, whether intentionally or unintentionally. Sometimes we hurt those who love us most by our defence mechanisms. We become self-centred, we withdraw, we put up walls, we live in our own world, we are impatient, we blame others, and we lash out—all of which causes hurt and anxiety to those closest to us.

After I had forgiven those who had hurt me, I began to realize that I was also in need of forgiveness. I needed forgiveness from my husband for the hurt I caused him through misplaced anger while I was going through my healing journey. Tears filled his eyes when I asked for his forgiveness, and I saw for the first time a small glimpse of the emotional pain that he and my children had suffered in the previous years. I was in such extensive pain myself that I was unaware of the pain my family was experiencing. I needed to ask forgiveness of each of my children for the ways I neglected their needs while I was walking through my own valley of pain.

I needed forgiveness from God for the lies I had believed about Him, for my anger at Him, and for my rebellious heart. There was one other area that, although God had forgiven me twenty years previously, I had never forgiven myself. I now needed to receive for myself God's wonderfully relentless love, compassion, mercy, and forgiveness.

There was an additional problem with the relationship I had with that young man in high school. Not only was he an unbeliever and I had given in to his enticing, I still carried around guilt. He had been married before. He'd gotten married at age nineteen and after a short time separated from his wife, eight months before I met him. So at the tender age of seventeen I became first cousin to the woman the Pharisees threw at Jesus' feet in John 8. By Old Testament law, I deserved to be stoned. At least, that's what my emotions were telling me and I just couldn't shake the guilt. Although God had forgiven me years earlier, I had never accepted God's forgiveness.

Have mercy on me, O God, according to your unfailing love; according to your great compassion blot out my transgressions. Wash away all my iniquity and cleanse me from my sin. For I know my transgressions, and my sin is always before me. Against you, you only, have I sinned..." (Psalms 51:1–4)
The teachers of the law and the Pharisees brought in a woman caught in adultery. They made her stand before the group and said to Jesus, "Teacher, this woman was caught in adultery. In the law Moses commanded us to stone such a woman. Now what do you say?" They were using this question as a trap, in order to have a basis for accusing him. But Jesus bent down and started to write on the ground with his finger. (John 8:3–6)

When Jesus stooped down to write on the ground, He took time to quieten His heart and ask His Father how He should answer the Pharisees.

> *When they kept on questioning him, he straightened up and said to them, "If any one of you is without sin, let him be the first to throw a stone at her."*
> *Again he stooped down and wrote on the ground.* (John 8:7–8)

Jesus said only what He had to say, then kept quiet to allow the Holy Spirit to do His work of convicting these men.

> *At this, those who heard began to go away one at a time, the older ones first, until only Jesus was left, with the woman still standing there. Jesus straightened up and asked her, "Woman, where are they? Has no one condemned you?"*
> *"No one, sir," she said.*
> *"Then neither do I condemn you, [Grace,]" Jesus declared. "Go now and leave your life of sin."* (John 8:9–11)

God embraces those whom religious people judge and throw away.
The Bible doesn't tell us what Jesus wrote. Possibly He listed the Pharisees' sins:

> *Honor your father and your mother... You shall not murder. You shall not commit adultery. You shall not steal. You shall not give false testimony against your neighbour. You shall not covet your neighbour's wife... or anything that belongs to your neighbor.* (Deuteronomy 5:16–21)

Maybe Jesus wrote words of compassion for this woman. Possibly He quoted the prophet, Jeremiah:

> *I have loved you with an everlasting love; I have drawn you with loving-kindness, I will build you up again and you will be rebuilt.* (Jeremiah 31:3–4)

"For I know the plans I have for you," declares the Lord, "plans to prosper you and not to harm you, plans to give you hope and a future." (Jeremiah 29:11)

Maybe Jesus quoted Isaiah:

Though your sins are like scarlet, they shall be as white as snow; though they are red as crimson, they shall be like wool. (Isaiah 1:18)

It's not important what Jesus wrote. If it were, those words would have been recorded for us to read. The important thing is that Jesus stooped down. Jesus left His home in heaven and became a man—a perfect, sinless man—so that He could take our sins to the cross and leave them there. In Psalm 18:35, the psalmist lifts his heart in praise as he exclaims, *"You stoop down to make me great."* God took on the form of man so that man might put on the character of God.

Jesus waded into the muck, stooped down, tenderly lifted me into His arms, carried me out, set my feet on a solid rock, and gave me a firm place to stand. He never scolded me. He quieted me with His love and said, *"I will heal [your] waywardness and love [you] freely, [Grace]"* (Hosea 14:4).

Forgiveness, whether given or received, isn't easy. It's hard work and very costly. It goes against our natural instincts and is an assault to our pride and will, both in asking for forgiveness and granting it. We want to make sure the offender has suffered sufficiently before we let him off the hook. We are afraid that if we forgive too quickly, we will suffer the same hurt again. If we are the one in need of forgiveness, we may be afraid of committing the same offence or make excuses for our behaviour.

The key is that we can't do it in our own strength; we need the help of our Heavenly Father, who knows more than anyone the cost of forgiveness. Forgiveness cost God the Father the death of His Son, Jesus.

HOW FORGIVEN IS FORGIVEN?

Does God keep score? Does He keep all our past confessed offences in His back pocket ready to pull out the next time we sin against Him?

What exactly does God do with our confessed sins? Here's what the Bible tells us.

If we confess our sins, he is faithful and just and will forgive us our sins and purify us from all unrighteousness. (1 John 1:9)

God not only forgives our sins, He cleanses us so that we are just as pure as if we had never sinned.

As far as the east is from the west, so far has he removed our transgressions from us. (Psalm 103:12)

How far is the east from the west? If you travel east or west you can travel forever and ever and never come to an end.

Surely it was for my benefit that I suffered such anguish. In your love you kept me from the pit of destruction; you have put all my sins behind your back. (Isaiah 38:17)

If something is behind our backs, we can't see it. God chooses not to look at our sins after he has forgiven us.

You will again have compassion on us; you will tread our sins underfoot and hurl all our iniquities into the depths of the sea. (Micah 7:19)

When something is dropped into the deepest part of the ocean, it is unreachable. It is gone forever.

I, even I, am he who blots out your transgressions, for my own sake, and remembers your sins no more. (Isaiah 43:25)

Often when we have asked God to forgive our sins we still feel guilty so we ask Him to forgive us again and again and again. But when we ask for forgiveness a second or third time, God says, "I don't remember you doing that."

Blessed is he whose transgressions are forgiven, whose sins are covered. (Psalm 32:1)

Be imitators of God therefore,
as dearly loved children.
(Ephesians 5:1)

The Process of Forgiveness

The Lord is My Helper

I lift up my eyes to the hills—
where does my help come from?
My help comes from the Lord,
the Maker of heaven and earth.
He will not let your foot slip.

The cords of death entangled me;
the torrents of destruction overwhelmed me.
The cords of the grave coiled around me;
the snares of death confronted me.
In my distress I called to the Lord; I cried to my God for help.
From his temple he heard my voice;
my cry came before him, into his ears.
He reached down from on high and took hold of me;
he drew me out of deep waters.
He rescued me from my powerful enemy,
from my foes, who were too strong for me.
The Lord was my support.
He brought me out into a spacious place;
he rescued me, because he delighted in me.

I waited patiently for the Lord;
he turned to me and heard my cry.
He lifted me out of the slimy pit,
out of the mud and mire;
he set my feet on a rock and gave me a firm place to stand.
He put a new song in my mouth,
a hymn of praise to our God.
Many will see and fear and put their trust in the Lord.

Help us, O God our Saviour,
for the glory of your name;
deliver us and forgive our sins for your name's sake.

My flesh and my heart may fail,
but God is the strength of my heart.
For the eyes of the Lord range throughout the earth
to strengthen those whose hearts are fully committed to Him.
Those who hope in the Lord will renew their strength.
The Lord is my strength and my shield;
my heart trusts in Him, and I am helped.
Look to the Lord and His strength;
seek His face always.
Remember the wonders He has done.
I can do everything through Him who gives me strength.

God has said, "Never will I leave you;
never will I forsake you."
So we say with confidence,
"The Lord is my helper; I will not be afraid.
What can man do to me?"
So do not fear, for I am with you;
do not be dismayed,
for I am your God.
I will strengthen you and help you;
I will uphold you with my righteous right hand.
For I am the Lord, your God,
who takes hold of your right hand and says to you,
"Do not fear; I will help you. Do not be afraid,
for I myself will help you," declares the Lord.

We wait in hope for the Lord;
he is our help and our shield.
God is our refuge and strength,
an ever-present help in trouble.
Therefore we will not fear.[36]

---

36 Paraphrased from Psalms 121:1–3; Psalms 18:4–6,16–19; Psalms 40:1–3; Psalms 79:9; Psalms 73:26; 2 Chronicles 16:9; Isaiah 40:31; Psalms 28:7; 1 Chronicles 16:11–12; Philippians 4:13; Hebrews 13:5–6; Isaiah 41:10, 13–14; Psalms 33:20; and Psalms 46:1–2.

CHAPTER
Twenty-two

RESTORATION

*"I will restore you to health
and heal your wounds,"
declares the Lord.*
(Jeremiah 30:17)

WHEN A RELATIONSHIP IS BEING RESTORED, IT NEEDS TO BE PROTECTED so that the same offence doesn't occur again. Setting boundaries can help make both parties feel safe in the relationship. However, someone who has never had boundaries and struggles with dependencies will find it difficult at first to set boundaries and stick with them. It will take determination and much trial and error, but setting boundaries is a must if we are going to maintain healthy relationships.

There is often some confusion between building walls and setting boundaries. A person who builds a wall does it to protect themselves from enduring more pain. The problem is that they not only shut out the people who would hurt them, but they also shut out interaction with people who want to love them and care for them. It is very difficult to get your emotional needs met by talking over a six-foot wall or peeking through a knothole. We all need emotional intimacy with trustworthy people, but fear often prevents us from opening up and entering into a close relationship.

In *The DNA of Relationships for Couples*, the idea of erecting walls is discussed.

> If you are like us, you long for relationships in which you feel completely safe. You want to feel free to open up and reveal who you really are and know that the other person will still love, accept and value you—no matter what. Yet many of us struggle with various aspects of intimacy because it requires openness, and openness makes us instantly vulnerable. We're not quite sure what others will say or do, or how they will use what they learn about us. This is why a lack of desire to connect—or an avoidance of intimacy in general—usually has to do with attempting to avoid pain, humiliation, embarrassment, or just plain discomfort. As a way to lower the risk, people come up with many strategies to try to connect without getting hurt. We put up walls and try to project an image we think people want.[37]

Then there is the contrast where the person, male or female, wants so desperately to be loved that they will hand their heart over to just about anyone, hoping against hope that this person will cherish it and not break it. This leaves them open to being used and taken advantage of in any number of ways—financially, emotionally, mentally, physically, or sexually—and then thrown away when the person is done with them. These are the people who stagger from one dysfunctional relationship to another, from dependency to dependency.

---

37 Smalley, Dr. Greg and Dr. Robert S. Paul. *The DNA of Relationships for Couples* (Wheaton, IL: Tyndale House Publishers, 2006), p. 57.

People pleasers can also be in leadership roles, where they fret constantly about disappointing people and as a result get taken advantage of and emotionally manipulated for their time and energy. These individuals end up burning out. This was part of where my weakness lay in ministry. I had not set firm boundaries, so people often took advantage of my time and energy.

The better choice would be to set boundaries. Like building walls, their purpose is for protection, but that's where the similarity ends. Boundaries are more like a three-foot fence with a gate (an analogy which I borrow from a Joyce Meyer sermon). The fence allows face-to-face interaction and also limited physical touch. When you have established that this person is trustworthy, you have the option of inviting him or her into a deeper relationship through the gate. Similarly, if this person proves not to be trustworthy, you can take a step back and close the gate until you can feel safe with him or her again.

I found the book *Boundaries* very helpful in learning to set safe boundaries for myself.

Boundaries affect all areas of our lives:
- Physical boundaries help us determine who may touch us, how, and when.
- Mental boundaries give us freedom to have our own thoughts and opinions.
- Emotional boundaries help us deal with our own emotions and disengage us from the harmful, manipulative emotions of others.
- Spiritual boundaries help us distinguish God's will from our own and give us renewed awe for our Creator.[38]

Boundaries help us to know when to say "yes" and when to say "no" and to take control of our own life.[39]

---

38 Cloud, Dr. Henry and Dr. John Townsend. *Boundaries* (Grand Rapids, MI: Zondervan, 1992), back cover.
39 Ibid., front cover.

Boundaries define us. They define what is me and what is not me. A boundary shows me where I end and someone else begins, leading me to a sense of ownership.[40]
Setting boundaries inevitably involves taking responsibility for your choices.[41]

Setting boundaries allowed me to have freedom from owning another person's guilt and shame. It meant that, although I had been abused, it was not my shame to own but the person who committed the crime. When someone in my family did something that was hurtful, I could step back and not own their actions or consequences.

All choices have consequences; poor choices have negative consequences and good, healthy choices have positive consequences. Boundaries basically say that I will take responsibility for myself, and you will take responsibility for yourself. I can be supportive and share your burden, but I won't own your mistakes or carry your load. The apostle Paul put it this way: *"Carry each other's burdens... [but]each one should carry his own load"* (Galatians 6:2, 5).

After so many years of taking responsibility for other people's actions, I found it very difficult to break free from the old tapes that played in my mind and the disapproval of friends and family. It meant starting over to build a different foundation for relationships that would require earning trust and making commitments by all individuals concerned.

The DNA of Relationships for Couples gives us a definition of what trustworthiness should look like:

You are trustworthy when you fully grasp how valuable and vulnerable another person is, and you treat that person accordingly. To the extent that you treat the person as precious and irreplaceable, you are trustworthy. And to the extent that you don't, you're not.[42]

---

40 Ibid., p. 29.
41 Ibid., p. 43.
42 Smalley, Dr. Greg and Dr. Robert S. Paul. *The DNA of Relationships for Couples* (Wheaton, IL: Tyndale House Publishers, 2006), p. 75.

Similarly, the other person is trustworthy only as long as he or she demonstrates their appreciation for your value.

There are two commitments you can make yourself:

• Commitment #1: Commit yourself to being trustworthy.
• Commitment #2: Require others to be trustworthy toward you.[43]

Proverbs 4:23 provides some great wisdom on setting boundaries and requiring people to be trustworthy: *"Above all else, guard your heart, for it is the wellspring of life."*

When you have boundaries, you are trustworthy to yourself. You are able to step back when someone behaves badly toward you, and protect that valuable, vulnerable part of yourself,

> like drawing a line in the sand and saying, "Hey, I'm safeguarding this part of me because I can't trust you with it right now. But I do want to have a relationship with you. Therefore, I will give you repeated opportunities to try again. But I need you to know that the next time I let you in, and every single time thereafter, I'll be requiring the same thing: that you show me, through words and actions, that you understand how valuable and vulnerable I am and that you act accordingly. To the degree that you do this, let's be friends. But when you forget, I need you to know that I won't forget.

Your ability to feel safe in a relationship depends more on the second part of trustworthiness than on the first. When we remain trustworthy to ourselves, we can afford to give others a lot of freedom in relationships. We know that others are going to forget, that they are going to have moments when they stop being trustworthy. We can live with that, however, because there's always someone taking responsibility—we are. When other people act in unsafe ways, when they get caught up in themselves, we take the most vulnerable part of ourselves back

---

43 Ibid., p. 87.

and protect it. And when they regain their trustworthiness, we can say, "Let's try this again."[44]

> *Above all else,*
> *guard your heart,*
> *for it is the wellspring of life.*
> Proverbs 4:23

---

44 Ibid., pp. 86–87.

CHAPTER
Twenty-three

RESTORING MY RELATIONSHIPS

The wise woman builds her house,
but with her own hands
the foolish one
tears hers down.
(Proverbs 14:1)

AFFIRMING MY CHILDREN

I COMMITTED MYSELF TO PROVIDING A HEALTHY ENVIRONMENT FOR MY children. I devoted myself to helping my husband and children heal from the wounds my illness and dysfunctions had caused them.

I put into practice the five love languages—physical touch, words of affirmation, quality time, gifts, and acts of service—as discussed in *The Five Love Languages of Children.*

Even into their late teens and early twenties, I would sit and cuddle each child if they were hurting or if they just needed affection. I tried to express in every way possible the love that they needed in order to heal the hole in their hearts and give them back what they had lost in their formative years.

If one of my children came in from school and needed to talk, I dropped what I was doing and took the necessary time to listen to them. If one of them said, "Can you and I go to Tim Horton's tonight?" I knew they needed my time and I made myself available to them. I took every opportunity to let them express their emotions, be it sadness, anxiety, fear, or anger at me for causing them so much pain.

On one occasion when I stayed home from work with the flu, I felt so ill that I didn't get dressed all day, and when my one daughter arrived home from school she found me sitting in my bathrobe looking rather miserable. She became very irritated with me and made some hurtful comments. I let it go for a while and then later sat down with her to ask about what she was feeling. She said she was angry with me but didn't know why. After we talked for a while, I realized that she had flashed back to when I had been in a deep depression and sat around all day in that same bathrobe, with my hair a mess. I wrapped her in my arms and assured her I only had the flu and would be going back to work tomorrow. Then I took that bathrobe, chucked it in the garbage, and sat down to write the following poem.

A Mother's Regrets

My dear child:
If I'd known how to love,
I would have loved you better.
If I'd known how to hug,
you wouldn't have longed for my touch.

If my mother had had
an affectionate, caring, nurturing mother,
you would have had
an affectionate, caring, nurturing mother too.

My heart breaks,
to hear of your childhood loneliness.
You have every right
to feel angry, resentful, and hurt.
I was not meeting your needs.

Oh to turn back the years,
to heal your aching heart.
I would take every chance
to do it all over again.

To take you in my lap,
to hold you in my arms,
to give you what you really wanted
and needed most from me: my love.
Love Always and Forever,
Mom

REBUILDING MY MARRIAGE

I was raised in an environment where I survived by keeping secrets, pretending everything was okay and not making waves. It was a place where pain was made fun of and tears were hidden by laughter. My husband was raised in a home where he was taught that one gets his own way by manipulation, and failing that by anger and fits of rage.

My marriage required more than just a makeover; it needed reconstructing from the foundation up. This was not an easy task after thirteen years of a codependent marriage, where I was needy and he needed to be needed. Two broken people can never make a whole marriage. One person does not complete the other. When we look to someone else to fulfill us or meet our needs, we are expecting more than that person can deliver. God is the only one who can complete a person and bring about wholeness.

We had both married for the happiness we thought our partner could give us. In reading *The DNA of Relationships for Couples*, I discovered the problem with marrying for happiness.

> Perhaps the most problematic myth we hear is this: If you are not happy with your marriage, you may have married the wrong person.
> A marriage is in big trouble when happiness is the goal. If happiness or finding your soul mate is the objective, this is a huge setup for failure—or at least years of frustration. This is such a setup, because what happens when you're not happy? What does the absence of happiness mean? It makes you wonder whether you may have married the wrong person or if there is something wrong with you or your mate.[45]

I had become an extension of my husband and forfeited my own identity. Learning to set boundaries helped me look after my own health first by discovering that it was okay to say "no." I learned that although I was married, I was still an individual, separate from my husband. I

---

45 Ibid., p. 124.

was entitled to my own thoughts, opinions, ideas, and emotions. It was okay to disagree with his way of thinking. I learned to take responsibility for my own behaviour and assign my husband to take responsibility for his. Sometimes that meant stepping back and allowing him to make mistakes and reaping the consequences for them.

While all of these changes were good for me, they threw my husband into confusion, as I was no longer the person he had married. When I began to heal and change and become more independent, my husband felt threatened and insecure. He became fearful of losing me, consequently pressing his fear buttons. He tried to manipulate me with an overabundance of affection. But that made me feel suffocated and I pushed him away.

So while I struggled for freedom and individuality, he held on tighter and tried to control, resulting in pressing my fear buttons. I felt overpowered and fought back, while he needed to have his feelings validated.

Consequently he pulled out his other trusty weapons. But by this time in my healing journey, I had developed some new talent of my own, so I met anger with anger and rage with rage. I think those earth tremors we felt back then were actually started by us.

The fear only escalated further. Thus we went many, many rounds with the Fear Dance, as described in *The DNA of Relationships*. We all have core fears that can trigger the Fear Dance in our relationships.[46]

We were like two boxers in a ring, dancing around each other looking for an opportunity to get our punch in. He would throw his verbal accusations at me and I would come back swinging with my own. Around and around we went, trying to get the other person to change so that our own wants and needs could be met. Eventually one of us would walk away to gather our thoughts and come up with more ammunition for the next round.

Our marriage was going from bad to worse and neither of us knew how to stop the Fear Dance. We both wanted to save our marriage but were helpless to know how to do that. If we could have had access to *The DNA of Relationships* back then, we would have had some helpful

46 Ibid., p. 45.

answers, as the book goes on to describe how to put in place new dance steps of relating to each other. These new steps involve realizing that you cannot change the other person. You can only, with God's help, change yourself and how you respond when your fear buttons get pushed.

We both took our concerns to prayer and read whatever we could find on repairing our marriage. We took a weekend away by ourselves and while we were there my husband showed me a book he was reading by Stormie Omartian entitled *The Power of a Praying Husband*.[47] He began reading some excerpts from it. When we returned home, I bought Stormie's book, *The Power of a Praying Wife*.[48] We began praying for each other's emotional needs and fears through the chapters of these books, and before long we saw changes in the way we related to each other. We learned to listen with sensitivity to the other's feelings and communicate in an unthreatening manner. We were then able to express our fears and emotional needs in a healthier way.

The DNA of Relationships for Couples describes where we began to see ourselves in our relationship.

> An alternative to the happily-ever-after fantasy is to see marriage as a journey. The truth is that happiness is nice, but marriage is more about choosing a journeying partner than finding your soul mate. What's good about having a journey perspective is that a journey contains both the good and the bad. It contains the mountain-top experiences and the valleys. So if you make your goal about journeying together instead of about happiness, you allow the marriage to contain both the happy times and the painful times, without seeing the negatives as problematic. Both are expected and accepted…
>
> …If you look at the decision to marry as actually the choosing of a journey partner with the goal of growing into a more perfect representation of the man and woman you were both created

---

47 Omartian, Stormie. *The Power of a Praying Husband* (Eugene, OR: Harvest House Publishers, 1997).
48 Omartian, Stormie. *The Power of a Praying Wife* (Eugene, OR: Harvest House Publishers, 1997).

to become, then the evaluation of your marriage takes on a different slant. From this perspective, marriage becomes a series of three simultaneous journeys, each with its own objectives and responsibilities.... The three journeys are...

My Journey

My Spouse's Journey

The Marriage Journey[49]

Without having these wonderful words of wisdom (as they hadn't been written yet), the Lord led my husband and me along this path of healing. First, I was for the most part finished my healing journey and was growing and changing as an individual. Secondly, I was supporting and encouraging my husband on his healing journey toward growth and change. Thirdly, we were both working hard on restoring our marriage. There were many obstacles along the way, but we were both determined to make it work.

One evening while my husband and I were sitting listening to music, he pulled up the song "Never My Love," by The Association, on the internet and sang it to me:

By the time he finished singing the song, tears were streaming down my face.

He printed off the song and read it to me again. Then the gentle voice of my Heavenly Father spoke to my heart and said that I had never truly believed that my husband would love me for the rest of his life. Subconsciously, I had always thought he would get tired of me and move on to someone else. I had never believed I was deserving of his love.

My Heavenly Father had that song come to my husband's mind and impressed it on him to sing it to me, because that was what I needed to hear. This was yet another wonderful sign of my Father's and husband's love for me.

Years later, my son was home from university for the weekend. He walked into the kitchen while my husband and I were sharing a special moment. After his father left the room, my son said, "That man loves

---

49 Smalley, Dr. Greg and Dr. Robert S. Paul. *The DNA of Relationships for Couples* (Wheaton, IL: Tyndale House Publishers, 2006), p. 125.

you more than I have ever seen anyone love anybody. If there is one thing Dad has taught us kids, it's how a man ought to love his wife." To that I responded, "I am beyond doubt a blessed woman."

Lord, you have assigned me my portion and my cup;
you have made my lot secure.
The boundary lines have fallen for me in pleasant places;
surely I have a delightful inheritance.
(Psalms 16:5–6)

Praise awaits you, O God, in Zion;
to you our vows will be fulfilled.
(Psalm 65:1)

CHAPTER
Twenty-four

OVERFLOWING WITH HOPE

I waited patiently for the Lord; he turned to me and heard my cry.
He lifted me out of the slimy pit, out of the mud and the mire;
he set my feet on a rock and gave me a firm place to stand.
He put a new song in my mouth, a hymn of praise to our God.
Many will see and fear and put their trust in the Lord.
(Psalms 40:1–3)

SHARING MY EXPERIENCE

EARLY IN MY HEALING JOURNEY, AS I WAS STUDYING MY BIBLE, I WAS struck by the following words: *"For it has been granted to you on behalf of Christ not only to believe on him, but also to suffer for him"* (Philippians 1:29). I wondered why those words leapt off the page at me. I read them over several times and then asked my Heavenly Father what this verse had to do with me at this point in my life. I had always thought this verse referred to being persecuted for my faith. It impressed upon me the great privilege it is to suffer for the cause of our Saviour and Lord.

But the Spirit was now telling me that my healing journey was going to be a means of suffering for Christ. I was being entrusted with a special experience with which I was to reach out to other hurting people. I was to tell my story. I was to allow myself to be vulnerable and transparent so that countless emotional prisoners could be set free.

Picture an empty pitcher with a network of cracks down the front. Now imagine that pitcher filled with light and a lid put on the top. Where does the light shine through? The cracks. That is the way the Lord's light shines through our lives. Not so much by what we do well naturally, but by what He must do in us supernaturally for it to be so.[50]

I wasn't to turn the cracks of my life toward the wall so that others wouldn't know the truth about me. God never intended for me to be a closet survivor. I was to be visible so that God's light could shine through the cracks of my life. *"My grace is sufficient for you, for my power is made perfect in weakness"* (2 Corinthians 12:9).

As I listened to the Spirit speak to my heart, a dream began to take shape, a dream that I would one day use my healing journey to help many other wounded people. I was to write a book, and as I prayed about a name for my book, the title *From Victim to Victor* came to me.

Other verses throughout my healing journey were given to me as a promise toward my dream.

[Grace, Grace,] Satan has asked to sift you as wheat. But I have prayed for you, [Grace,] that your faith may not fail. And when you have turned back, strengthen your brothers. (Luke 22:31, emphasis added)

Praise be to the God and Father of our Lord Jesus Christ, the Father of compassion and the God of all comfort, who comforts us in all our troubles, so that we can comfort those in any trouble with

---

50 Clairmont, Patsy. *God Uses Cracked Pots* (Nashville, TN: Word Publishing, 1991), p. 1.

the comfort we ourselves have received from God. *For just as the sufferings of Christ flow over into our lives, so also through Christ our comfort overflows.* (2 Corinthians 1:3–5, emphasis added)

May the God of hope fill you with all joy and peace as you trust in him, so that you may overflow with hope *[to other wounded people] by the power of the Holy Spirit.* (Romans 15:13, emphasis added)

[Grace] will be like a shelter *from the wind and a refuge from the storm [for other wounded people], like streams of water in the desert and the shadow of a great rock in a thirsty land [where others may be refreshed].* (Isaiah 32:2, emphasis added)

At the beginning of my healing journey, after I had been in the psychiatric ward for several days, a woman, Sharon, was brought into the bed next to mine. I was sitting on my bed reading my Bible when Sharon began asking me questions about my faith. I felt like such a failure that I didn't think I could witness to her. How does someone who has just hit bottom with a splat witness to anyone? How could I say that if it weren't for God, I wouldn't be where I am today? So I just passed along to her the verses God was giving me to comfort my heart.

After I was discharged, I kept in touch with her, passing along the verses God was giving me as I searched for healing. I put in some verses on how to become a child of God as well.[51] Several weeks later, Sharon called me and told me that she was born again. She had read the verses of God's love for her and His plan of salvation and had given her life to the Lord.

As our friendship grew, Sharon told me that when she first saw me sitting on my bed reading my Bible, she had said to herself, *God must really be mad at me this time; He has put me in a room with a Bible thumper.* Sharon also told me that although it was evident that I was in a great deal of emotional pain when she first met me, she could still see an underlying peace and strength. God shines even through our brokenness; in fact, that's when He shines best.

---

51 Please see Appendix A, "How to Become a Child of God."

This was a confirmation of God's love for me. Even at my lowest point, when I thought I had messed up so badly that God was finished with me, God used me to reach Sharon. He had placed me in the next bed to Sharon so that she could hear of God's love for her. God's amazing, isn't He?

Sharon is admitted to hospital two or three times a year for medication changes. While she's there, she spends her time sharing God's love with the other patients.

I took all that I had learned through my healing process and shared it with my husband and children so that they could grow and heal as individuals. I shared my verses on God's love for us. Each week, we would study a new verse and memorize it so that it could take root in the emotional level of our lives. I wanted my family to know deep within their emotions that their Heavenly Father loves them. The message I desperately tried to get across was:

- His love never wavers. There is nothing you can do to diminish His love for you.
- He is never disappointed in you.
- He is not angry with you.
- He takes great delight in you.
- He rejoices over you with singing.
- He calls you His treasured possession.
- He says you are precious and honoured in His sight.
- He comforts you with His love.
- He carries you in His arms when you are weak or hurting.
- He longs for fellowship with you.
- He delights to give good gifts to you.

Toward the end of my five-year healing journey, I organized a support group for wounded women. I shared with them the many verses God had given me through my healing process. I also shared the steps I went through, and the tools I used, so that they could use them in their own journey.

REBUILDING THE WALLS OF OUR LIVES
(NEHEMIAH 1–3)

The emotional scars of our childhood, the loss of relationships, and the death of loved ones all cause a breakage in the walls of our lives. They leave us feeling vulnerable and exposed to reoccurrences of abuse and emotional wounds. We need to rebuild. But before we rebuild, we need to allow ourselves time to mourn and grieve our losses. We need help and guidance from God and the support of friends and family to put the pieces of our lives back together. Nehemiah is a wonderful example of how to go about rebuilding the walls of our lives.

"The wall of Jerusalem is broken down, and its gates have been burned with fire. When I heard these things, I sat down and wept. For some days I mourned and fasted and prayed..." (Nehemiah 1:3–4).

Give yourself permission to take time to feel your emotions. Take time to pour out your heart to God.

"For some days I mourned and fasted and prayed... I went to Jerusalem, and [stayed] there three days [in prayer]" (Nehemiah 1:4, 2:11).

Ask God to guide you on your healing journey. Ask Him to show you whom you can trust to keep your confidence.

"I set out [secretly] during the night with a few men. I had not told anyone what God had put in my heart to do" (Nehemiah 2:12).

Gather support through dependable prayer partners. Ask a couple of trustworthy, supportive people whom you are comfortable with to hold you up in prayer as you work through your healing process.

"By night [privately] I went out... examining the walls of Jerusalem, which had been broken down, and its gates, which had been destroyed by fire" (Nehemiah 2:13).

Examine the damages with dependable friends and/or a counsellor. Examine the painful memories.

"You see the trouble we are in: Jerusalem lies in ruins, and its gates have been burned with fire" (Nehemiah 2:17).

My life is devastated and my boundaries have been violated.

"The officials did not know where I had gone or what I was doing, because as yet I had said nothing to [anyone]" (Nehemiah 2:16).

Prayerfully set your boundaries. Keep your confidences within your circle of supporters to assure that you won't become a topic of gossip.

"'Come, let us rebuild the wall of Jerusalem and we will no longer be in disgrace'... They replied, 'Let us start rebuilding'" (Nehemiah 2:17–18).

Commit to healing. Ask your group of supporters to commit to helping you work through the damages that have been done so that you can become a healthy, confident person.

"I also told them about the gracious hand of my God upon me" (Nehemiah 2:18).

Identify God's hand at work in each small step of growth and healing. Share with your group the verses, books, and other healing aids that God gives you so that they are encouraged and God is glorified in your healing process.

"They mocked and ridiculed us. 'What is this you are doing?' they asked. 'Are you rebelling against the king?'" (Nehemiah 2:19)

Expect opposition. Friends and family who are comfortable with your previous dysfunctions will not want you to change. What is in the past stays in the past; don't go dragging it up. Stop feeling sorry for yourself. Family members may verbally or nonverbally imply, "Do not tell anyone about our family secrets. This is the way we have always interacted and we are not going to change now."

"The God of heaven will give us success. We his servants will start rebuilding" (Nehemiah 2:20).

"Trust in the Lord with all your heart and lean not on your own understanding; in all your ways acknowledge him, and he will make your paths straight" (Proverbs 3:5–6).

Trust God for the outcome. Just do the work of healing. God will do His part in healing you and help you overcome the obstacles that trip you up along the way.

"The high priest and his fellow priests went to work and rebuilt the Sheep Gate. They dedicated it..." (Nehemiah 3:1)

Dedicate the progress to God. With each small step of healing, take time to thank God and give Him glory for the progress. Ask Him to help you use what you are learning as you heal, to give hope to other wounded people.

"Set its doors in place" (Nehemiah 3:1).

Reset healthy boundaries for relationships. When the boundaries are built, put the doors in place so that you can control who has access to your life. You need only let in people who are trustworthy.

THE ROAD TOWARD HEALING

1. I committed myself to doing the work. I made getting well my full-time job.
2. I prayed daily for healing and had several people praying for me as well.
3. I studied Scripture to find out who God is and how He feels about me as His child. I totally immersed myself in Scripture, believing that God would use it to transform my mind.
4. In my journal, I examined individual verses—line by line, phrase by phrase, and word by word—as I personalized them, interacted with them (out loud), and applied them to my life. I found this way of studying very helpful in getting the Word into the deepest level of my emotions. (It has been scientifically proven that people tend to believe more of what they hear themselves say, out loud, than what they hear anyone else say.)

5. I went back and revisited my old wounds with a counsellor.

6. I forgave those who had hurt me. I asked God and my family to forgive me, I accepted their forgiveness, and I forgave myself.

7. I wrote in my journal about my feelings relating to my healing journey and everyday situations.

8. I played praise music while I was trying to get to sleep so that my thoughts were kept under control.

9. I studied, underlined, and made notes on many, many books on various topics and issues concerning my healing journey. These books were personal stories, or were written by counsellors, doctors, or pastors, giving counsel on various topics and treatments that worked for them.

10. I listened to tapes with helpful sermons for my situation.

11. I meditated on and committed to memory verses on God's love for me. I carried my list of verses with me wherever I went so that I could read and meditate on them (out loud whenever possible), whether going for a walk, riding on the bus, or waiting for appointments.

12. I did word searches in Scripture on my individual needs and issues—love, comfort, hope, healing, anger, forgiveness, and many other topics—using a concordance. (Now that I have a computer and the internet, I simply type my topic into Biblegateway.com and get all the verses in the Bible on that topic. I then read through them and copy and paste the ones most helpful to me into a Word document to use as a Bible study).

13. I organized these verses into scripture collages and gave them out to other hurting people.

You are to help your brothers
until the Lord gives them rest
as he has done for you,
and until they too
have taken possession of the land
that the Lord your God is giving them
[until they too are living the abundant life].
(Joshua 1:14-15)

CHAPTER Twenty-five

LIVING THE VICTORIOUS LIFE

I press on to take hold
of that for which Christ Jesus took hold of me.
(Philippians 3:12)

"GOD, IF THIS PAIN IS FOR THE PURPOSE OF TRANSFORMING ME INTO YOUR likeness, STOP! The cost is too great." These were the words I sobbed at the beginning of my healing journey, and my Heavenly Father graciously gave me peace for a short while before the healing process continued.

CREATED FOR HIS GLORY

At the end of my five-year healing journey, as I was preparing a Bible study for my support group, the Lord brought Isaiah 43:6–7 to my attention:

Bring my sons from afar and my daughters from the ends of the earth—everyone who is called by my name, whom I created for my glory, whom I formed and made.

I read it again. *"Whom I created for my glory."* Right there, staring me in the face, was my purpose in life. It was as though the Lord was saying, "Now Grace, it's not all about you. You are not the centre of the universe. In fact, it's not about you at all."

I grew up in a home where I was virtually invisible. No one paid much attention to me and I preferred it that way most of the time, because if no one knew I was there, it was less likely that I would get hurt. I had gone from that situation into a marriage where my husband called me from work two or three times throughout the day and wanted to know where I was and who I was with at all times. I was definitely the centre of my husband's universe.

When I was battling depression, everything our family did depended on how I was feeling that particular day. We couldn't plan ahead, because we never knew if I was going to be smiling and calm, or buried in bed trembling and crying, or ranting and raving about something that had upset me.

Suddenly, the Lord was giving me a reality check. *"Whom I created for my glory."* I kept saying this phrase over and over to myself. Then I put my name in the phrase: *"Grace, whom I created for my glory… Grace, whom I created for my glory… Grace, whom I created for my glory…"* I pondered this phrase for several days as I allowed the truth of the verse to penetrate my heart.

I asked myself questions like, "What does it mean to glorify God? What does it mean for God to be glorified in my life?" I did some research and found that glorifying God means reflecting His character qualities in my life.

I looked up the word "reflect" in the dictionary and found—

1. to bend or cast back (as in light, heat, or sound).
2. to give back a likeness or image of as a mirror does.[52]

---

52 *Webster's New Explorer Dictionary* (Springfield, MA: Federal Street Press, 1999), p. 440.

I considered that if I was to give a reflection, then I must act as a reflector. I looked up the word "reflector" and found—

1. one that reflects.
2. a polished surface for reflecting radiation (as light).[53]

If an object is to be a reflector, it must have a smooth surface, not rough or warped. A calm lake gives a much better reflection than one with rough water.

I considered what this information meant to me as one whose purpose is to reflect God's character qualities. If I am to be an accurate reflection, then I must be clean and polished. The rough areas of my personality will need to be refined.

In thinking about reflections, I was reminded of a time when we took our children to a funhouse in Niagara Falls, Ontario. In one of the rooms, a wall was lined with mirrors reflecting distorted images. One mirror made you look tall and skinny, another made you look short and wide, and another made you look long in the body and short in the legs. There were many mirrors, each giving a different reflection. Although the object being reflected hadn't changed, the mirrors had distorted the image in direct relation to its own distortion.

Herein lies a truth: to the degree in which I am distorted in my belief about God and in my belief about myself as His child, I will distort the reflection I give of my Heavenly Father.

I had been looking into a warped mirror all of my life. I had believed a lie about God and myself as His child. It wasn't until I seriously began looking into the mirror of God's Word that I began to realize the truth. I am a child of God, His Spirit lives in my spirit, and I am loved by my Heavenly Father, but my emotional wounds prevented me from feeling the truth in my emotions.

I made another observation about my purpose as a reflector of God's character. If I am to give an accurate reflection, nothing must come between me and the source of light.

I thought about the lunar phases. The moon doesn't have any light of its own but reflects the light of the sun. The portion of the moon

---

53 Ibid.

that reflects the light of the sun each night is directly dependent on the relationship between the sun, the moon, and the earth.

Similarly, the degree to which I reflect the light of God depends on the relationship between the Son, me, and my world. To the extent that I let my world or my emotions and activities of life come between myself and the Son, Jesus, the reflection of God's character in my life will be diminished. But if I am in a right relationship with the Son, my reflection of the Father will be accurate.

Next, I looked into what God's character qualities are.

God is love. (1 John 4:16)

Love is patient, love is kind, it does not envy, it does not boast, it is not proud, it is not rude, it is not self-seeking, it is not easily angered, it keeps no record of wrongs. Love does not delight in evil but rejoices with the truth. It always protects, always trusts, always hopes, always perseveres. Love never fails. (1 Corinthians 13:4–8)

The fruit of the Spirit is love, joy, peace, patience, kindness, goodness, faithfulness, gentleness and self-control. (Galatians 5:22–23)

I thought of what it would be like to be able to reflect all of these wonderful attributes to people around me as I go about my day. I considered what the psalmist David expressed in Psalms 23:5. *"You anoint my head with oil [the Holy Spirit]; my cup overflows."* In a footnote from the Amplified Bible, it says,

Athletes anointed their bodies as a matter of course before running a race. As the body, therefore, anointed with oil was refreshed, invigorated and better fitted for action, so the Lord would anoint His "sheep" with the Holy Spirit Whom oil symbolizes, to fit them to engage more freely in His service and run in the way He directs, in heavenly fellowship with Him.[54]

_____

54 *The Amplified Bible* (Grand Rapids, MI: Zondervan, 1965), p. 627.

I pictured myself so full of the Holy Spirit that I bubbled over like a fountain, showering everyone around me with the fruit of the Spirit—love, joy, peace, patience, kindness, goodness, faithfulness, gentleness, and self-control. What an awesome picture!

I did some research to find other relating verses on glorifying God.

- In Ephesians 1:11–12, I read, *"In him we were also chosen... in order that we... might be for the praise of his glory."* So God created me and then saved me in order that I could bring praise to Him. He didn't save me primarily so that I could spend eternity in heaven, although that is part of the plan. God's purpose in creating me and then saving me is so that I will have the power through His indwelling Spirit to live my life in such a way that God is glorified in my life right now. Everyday! As a result, other people will be drawn to Jesus.

- In Galatians 1:24, the apostle Paul stated, *"They praised God because of me."* I wrote in the margin of my Bible, "Do people praise God because of me?" Isn't that my purpose, that people should praise God because of me?

- In Matthew 5:14–16, I learned more about the purpose of my healing journey. *"You are the light of the world. A city on a hill cannot be hidden. Neither do people light a lamp and put it under a bowl. Instead they put it on its stand, and it gives light to everyone in the house. In the same way, let your light shine before men, that they may see your good deeds and praise your Father in heaven."* When God gives a person a unique growing experience, He expects them to use it to help other people struggling with similar problems. The Holy Spirit was impressing upon me the need to tell the story of my healing journey so that others could be healed and glorify their Heavenly Father.

- In Psalms 19:1, I read, *"The heavens declare the glory of God; the skies proclaim the work of his hands."* The heavens declare the glory of God just by doing what God intended for it to do when He created it. The skies glorify God simply by fulfilling its purpose.

I was reminded of an entry that I had made in my journal several months previously. It had been dull and drizzly all day. The clouds hung dark and ominous. I had put off my daily walk because it looked like we were going to get a downpour at any moment. Then in the evening, as the sun began to set, the sky took on a whole new countenance. Those dark threatening clouds, now bathed in the light of the setting sun, were ribbons of deep purple floating in a sea of cotton candy pink. It was absolutely breathtaking.

As I stood awestruck, gazing up at the sunset, the Spirit spoke to my heart and said, "Just like the setting sun has turned these dark threatening clouds into a beautiful masterpiece, so shall I turn the dark clouds that have hovered over your life into a masterpiece of beauty and character. As you turn your face toward My Son, you also shall reflect My glory."

Gradually I began to realize the meaning of these words, *"Grace, whom I created for my glory."* God did not create me because He needed someone to talk to. He was capable of having a far more intelligent conversation with Himself. God created me to bring glory back to my creator and, like the skies, I do that by fulfilling the purpose for which I was created.

Joanne, whom I mentioned earlier, once asked me, "Why is it that we both come from the same background, and I became a prostitute, yet you didn't even sleep around?"

I thought for a moment and answered, "I think the difference between you and me is I had a praying mother. God in His grace chose to keep me from going down that path, but you He chose to save out of that way of life. I am no better than you are, Joanne. We are both products of God's grace and the best way we can thank Him is to live the rest of our lives for Him.

Be at rest once more, O my soul, for the Lord has been good to you.
For you, O Lord, have delivered my soul from death,
my eyes from tears, my feet from stumbling…
you have freed me from my chains.
(Psalms 116:7–8, 16)

THE PURPOSE OF PAIN IS CHANGE

The Lord will fulfill his purpose for me; your love O Lord, endures forever—do not abandon the works of your hands. (Psalms 138:8)

God uses the struggles in our lives to transform us and strengthen us for ministry. Supplementary difficulties are added, resulting in growth, transforming us into the likeness of His Son.

The real issue isn't whether things are going well for me or not. The important thing is how I weather the storms. Yet isn't pain and sorrow caused by sin? How can God be glorified through my suffering? Jesus' disciples had the same question. In John 9:1–3, we read,

As he went along, he saw a man blind from birth. His disciples asked him, "Rabbi, who sinned, this man or his parents, that he was born blind?"
"Neither this man nor his parents sinned," said Jesus, "but this happened so that the work of God might be displayed in his life."

How do I handle problems in my life? Do I whine and ask "Why me?" Do I gripe and complain and have a pity party? Do I compare my circumstances to someone else's? Do I get angry at God, or do I ask Him what He's going to do through this difficult situation? Do I ask God to bring glory to Himself through my problems? Do I surrender myself to God and ask Him to use this present pain to change me into His likeness? Do I choose to be bitter or better?

I consider that [my] present sufferings are not worth comparing with the glory that will be revealed in [me]… And we know that in all things God works for the good of those who love him… to be conformed to the likeness of his Son. (Romans 8:18, 28–29)

I have learned that what happens in my life really doesn't matter at all. What matters is that God be glorified in my life.

205

A veil covers their hearts. But whenever anyone turns to the Lord, the veil is taken away... And we, who with unveiled faces all reflect the Lord's glory, are being transformed [from the inside] into his likeness [a little at a time] with ever-increasing glory. (2 Corinthians 3:15–16, 18)

My forefathers had built for me a house on the sand. When the storms of life beat against my house, it collapsed, leaving me devastated. Through my healing journey, my Heavenly Father built for me a house on The Rock (Matthew 7:24–27).

He will be the sure foundation for your times,
a rich store of salvation and wisdom and knowledge;
the fear of the Lord [reverential trust, awe, respect, and worship]
is the key to this treasure.
(Isaiah 33:6)

Remember how the Lord your God led you all the way
[through your wilderness journey] in the desert these forty years,
to humble you and to test you in order to know what was in your heart...
He led you through the vast and dreadful desert [of emotional pain],
that thirsty and waterless land [of depression and loneliness],
with its venomous snakes and scorpions [of anger and fear]...
to humble and to test you so that in the end,
it might go well with you.
(Deuteronomy 8:2, 15–16)

SUFFERING FOR HIS PURPOSE

Do not be surprised at the painful trial you are suffering
as though something strange were happening to you.
But rejoice that you participate in the sufferings of Christ
so that you may be overjoyed when his glory is revealed [in you].

I am in pain and distress;
may your salvation, O God, protect me.
I will praise God's name in song
and glorify him with thanksgiving.
The poor will see and be glad—
you who seek God, may your hearts live!
The Lord hears the needy
and does not despise his captive people.

Consider it pure joy, my brothers,
whenever you face trials of many kinds,
because you know that the testing of your faith
develops perseverance.
Perseverance must finish its work
so that you may be mature and complete,
not lacking anything.

And the God of all grace,
who called you to his eternal glory in Christ,
after you have suffered a little while,
will himself restore you
and make you strong, firm and steadfast.

So do not throw away your confidence;
it will be richly rewarded.
You need to persevere
so that when you have done the will of God ,
you will receive what he has promised.

Being confident of this
that he who began a good work in you
will carry it on to completion
until the day of Christ Jesus.

He knows the way that I take;
when he has tested me,
I will come forth as gold.[55]

---

55 Paraphrased from 1 Peter 4:12–13; Psalms 69:29–30, 32–33; James 1:2–4;
1 Peter 5:10; Hebrews 10:35–36; Philippians 1:6; and Job 23:10.

CHAPTER
Twenty-six

MY SURE FOUNDATION

He will be the sure foundation for your times,
a rich store of salvation and wisdom and knowledge;
the fear of the Lord is the key to this treasure.
(Isaiah 33:6)

FIFTEEN YEARS AFTER MY WILDERNESS JOURNEY, I HAD AN OPPORTUNITY to see how much I had learned from this healing experience when God added some new verses to my new song.

He put a new song in my mouth, a hymn of praise to our God.
(Psalms 40:3)

They say that a perfect storm has two fronts that converge into one. I had three storms which converged in my life. Two had started three years previously, and then the third was added. If it hadn't been for the healing that had taken place in my life during my previous journey,

I never would have withstood this new earth-shattering experience. Although at times I was shaken totally to the core of my being and I developed serious physical ailments, my foundation of belief was solid and it stood firm.

I know who I am. I know whose I am. I know who my Father is. I know that I am loved by my Heavenly Father and I am carried in His arms. And I never once questioned His care for me.

Through my healing journey, God has changed me just like He promised He would.

I will sprinkle clean water on you, and you will be clean; I will cleanse you from all your impurities and from all your idols. I will give you a new heart and put a new spirit in you. I will remove from you your heart of stone and give you a heart of flesh. And I will put my Spirit in you and move you to follow my decrees and be careful to keep my laws... you will be my people, and I will be your God. I will save you from all your uncleanness. (Ezekiel 36:25–29)

My Heavenly Father has taken my cold stone heart that simply knew about His love and transformed it into one that not only feels His love but is deeply in love with Him. Through my healing process, God has given me compassion for wounded people and a desire to use my experience to help others.

Before my healing journey, I lived in a constant state of shock. I was so broken that I couldn't feel my emotions. I never felt deep sorrow or red hot anger, but neither could I feel great heights of joy or depths of love.

Someone once asked me if the pain of walking through my healing journey was worth it. My answer was yes. It was worth it... a thousand times worth it.

Although I keep close to my Shepherd these days, I do on the very rare occasion take a short daytrip without Him. But I am quick to come running back. There is no place on earth that remotely compares to the joy of living in His presence.

Recently, when I found myself overwhelmed with fear in a difficult situation, I did an inventory check on what I believe:

1. God is good. √
2. God loves me as His child. √
3. God desires to give good gifts to His children. √
4. The top three observations being true, have I in some area of my life wandered out from under God's umbrella of protection? √
5. If I am in a right relationship with my Heavenly Father, then the purpose for this present difficulty in my life must be that my Heavenly Father is inviting me to take our relationship to a higher level. √

Praise be to my Heavenly Father!

"For God, who said, 'Let light shine out of darkness,'
made his light shine in our hearts
to give us the light of the knowledge of the glory of God
in the face of Christ.
But we have this treasure in jars of clay
to show that this all-surpassing power is from God and not from us.
We are hard pressed on every side, but not crushed;
perplexed, but not in despair;
persecuted, but not abandoned;
struck down, but not destroyed…
so that the life of Jesus may also be revealed in our body…
For our light and momentary troubles
are achieving for us an eternal glory
that far outweighs them all."
(2 Corinthians 4:6–10, 17)

REFLECTIONS ON PSALM 103

"Praise the Lord, O my soul; all my inmost being, praise his holy name. Praise the Lord, O my soul, and forget not all his benefits..." (Psalms 103:1–2)

Father, I praise You with all that I am and have become; for what You have done in my life.

"...who forgives all your sins..." (Psalms 103:3)

You have cleansed me and forgiven me so that it is just as though I had never sinned, because the blood of Jesus continually cleanses me from all sin.

"...and heals all your diseases..." (Psalms 103:3)

You have set me free from the shadow of my past and healed my damaged emotions, because You are the Great Physician of body, soul, and spirit.

"...who redeems your life from the pit..." (Psalms 103:4)

You lifted me out of the slimy pit that I had fallen into and gave me a secure place to stand, in Your strength.

"...and crowns you with love and compassion..." (Psalms 103:4)

Father, You lift up my head as I find self-worth in You. You surround me with Your unfailing love and endless compassion.

"...who satisfies your desires with good things..." (Psalms 103:5)

You put Your desires for me into my heart so that I desire what You want for me.

"...so that your youth is renewed like the eagle's" (Psalms 103:5).

My childhood memories are healed and Your original design was restored. You have filled me with new hopes and dreams that enable me to soar with new excitement and passion.

"The Lord works righteousness and justice for all the oppressed" (Psalms 103:6).

Father, just as You have promised, You have brought good out of every sorrow and given me back blessings—double for my trouble.

"He made known his ways to Moses, his deeds to the people of Israel" (Psalms 103:7).

You also guide me in the paths that You would have me go.

"The Lord is compassionate and gracious, slow to anger, abounding in love" (Psalms 103:8).

Father, You have been continually merciful, forgiving, patient, and loving as I slowly, so very slowly, moved through my healing journey.

"He will not always accuse, nor will he harbor his anger forever" (Psalms 103:9).

You have disciplined me and restored me like a loving father corrects his child, and I am a better person because of it.

"He does not treat us as our sins deserve or repay us according to our iniquities" (Psalms 103:10).

You are forever merciful, forgiving, and patient with me.

"For as high as the heavens are above the earth, so great is his love for those who fear him" (Psalms 103:11).

Father, thank You that there is no end to Your love for me. You never run out of love for those who are trying to love, worship, and obey You.

"As far as the east is from the west, so far has he removed our sins from us" (Psalms 103:12).

With Your almighty arm, You have thrown my sins out into the universe where they will forever move away from me.

"As a father has compassion on his children, so the Lord has compassion on those who fear him…" (Psalms 103:13).

You never ask more of me than You will enable me to give or do. You never make a request of me that You do not give me the grace and strength to accomplish.

"…for he knows how we are formed, he remembers that we are dust" (Psalms 103:14).

You know how my personality was shaped. You know all the weaknesses of my humanity and You love me just as I am.

"As for man, his days are like grass, he flourishes like a flower of the field; the wind blows over it and it is gone, and its place remembers it no more" (Psalms 103:15–16).

Father, my life is but a vapour. Help me make every day count as I grow in the knowledge and likeness of Your Son, Jesus.

"But from everlasting to everlasting the Lord's love is with those who fear him, and his righteousness with their children's children— with those who keep his covenant and remember to obey his precepts" (Psalms 103:17–18).

Father, thank You for Your faithfulness. Please enable me to leave a legacy of Your love that will touch the hearts of generations to come.

"The Lord has established his throne in heaven, and his kingdom rules over all" (Psalms 103:19).

Nothing gets past you. You are always in control, even when bad things happen and I wonder why You have allowed it. Teach me to trust Your ever-encompassing wisdom, love, and plan for my life.

"Praise the Lord, you his angels, you mighty ones who do his bidding, who obey his word. Praise the Lord, all his heavenly hosts, you his servants who do his will. Praise the Lord, all his works everywhere in his dominion" (Psalms 103:20–22).

Father, please teach me to seek Your face for who You are, rather than Your hands for what You can do for me. Teach me to worship You with every ounce of my being.

Praise the Lord, O my soul!
(Psalms 103:22)

Praise the Lord, O my soul;
all my inmost being,
praise his holy name.
(Psalms 103:1)

IN HIS ARMS

Though pain and trials assault me,
And fear and loneliness haunt,
When I'm a lamb in the arms of my Shepherd,
There is nothing I need or want.

In the shadow of His hand He will keep me,
Until the raging storm is past.
I run to my place of refuge,
I'm safe in His arms at last.

Though my foe prowls around like a lion,
Not a threat from my enemy is heard.
When I'm wrapped in the arms of my Jesus,
I'm comforted by His words.

My child, there is much you have suffered,
But there is purpose in all I do.
I am moulding you into My likeness,
My image reflected in you.

Take courage My wounded child,
All is working out as I planned.
I'll never, never leave you,
You're engraved on the palms of My hands.[56]

---

56 Paraphrased from Isaiah 40:11; Isaiah 51:16; 1 Peter 5:8; Deuteronomy 33:12; Zephaniah 3:17; Job 36:15; 2 Corinthians 3:18; Jeremiah 29:11; Hebrews 13:5; and Isaiah 49:16.

Epilogue

BACK TO THE STONE QUARRY

I HAVE BEEN STUDYING GENE EDWARDS' BOOK, *THE INWARD JOURNEY*.[57] In it, he drives his point home over and over again: the purpose of pain is change. Pain and difficulty is often the way the Lord brings about change in our character. We can either choose brokenness or bitterness. If we choose brokenness, God is able to reshape us into the image of His Son, but if we choose bitterness we will have to take the same test over and over again until we learn the necessary lesson. The end result will be us becoming either bitterer or better. Our Heavenly Father is more interested in developing His character qualities in our lives than in our accomplishments according to the world's standards.

---

57 Edwards, Gene. *The Inward Journey* (Wheaton, IL: Tyndale House Publishers, 1993).

There is something very self-centered that will never die except for the jabbing pains of adversity. If you resist, if you hold on to that deep self-centered place, ever guarding it, making sure that it is not invaded even by the hand of God, then something in you will go unchanged and unbroken throughout all of your life upon this earth. An altar, a throne room, an inner sanctuary where self is worshiped will never be cast down. Be sure… one day the Lord will lift the hand of protection from you, and out of love he will say," Now I will allow this one to suffer."[58]

Something different is meted out to each of us. That which would cause absolutely no work of transformation in one Christian's life is an excruciating agony in another's… The suffering that befalls each of us is custom-made… At one time or another every one of us seems to cry out: "If it were just something else"… Tailor-made to do the deepest possible work and at the most inconvenient time, in the most vulnerable spot—that bears his fingerprint.[59]

The Lord will sometimes touch your spirit, sometimes it will be your soul, and sometimes it will be your body… Whatever it is the Lord puts into your life, that affliction is a friend working for you, not against you.[60]

The whole exercise of blame and resentment is a waste of time, accomplishing nothing. No matter how much fault you find in an other person, nor the amount of blame you charge him with, it is not going to change you.[61]

There is one thing you must not do. Complain if you must, groan if you must, and get angry if you must. But oh, dear brother, stay

---

58 Ibid., p. 65.
59 Ibid., p. 107.
60 Ibid., pp. 54–55.
61 Ibid., p. 112.

far distant from bitterness, and from blaming others. No matter what it is, don't blame others. Do that and you are dangerously close to forfeiting all future spiritual growth.[62]

What the Lord is doing in your life is toward this end: to make you as complete in Christ as any other saint who has ever lived, He is working the same thing in me. He has fashioned every circumstance that enters into your life toward that end. There are no accidental happenings in any Christian's life. His goal is to change you into his likeness.[63]

But why does God permit such suffering to befall his bride? This suffering produces gold in the lives of those individuals who suffer. That gold, in each life, is then blended into the body of Christ to make the bride what she ought to be... The very thing that you are now rebelling against just might be in perfect harmony with the Lord. What you see and feel so painfully may be the Lord's effort to polish a stone.[64]

Be sure, affliction that comes into your life carries with it a word from the Lord... Suffering from the Lord has a disciplinary effect upon the life of any believer. The Lord is seeking to transform every portion of the Bride of Christ so that her totality might be something that matches the very Son of God.[65]

No it is not what happens to you that is important. How you react to what it is... that's important. If your suffering is for Christ, and if your suffering is with Christ, the outcome will depend upon how your spirit faced up to your catastrophe.[66]

---

62 Ibid., p. 121.
63 Ibid., p. 142.
64 Ibid., p. 150.
65 Ibid., p. 54.
66 Ibid., p. 107.

Pain and sorrow in this world is inevitable. Jesus said, *"In this world you will have trouble. But take heart! I have overcome the world"* (John 16:33).

The hammer of pain, the chisel of illness, and the buffeting of relationships we experience in this life are all really just a reminder that we are still in the stone quarry. But this too shall pass.

And I—in righteousness I will see your face;
when I awake [in glory],
I will be satisfied with seeing your likeness [in me].
(Psalm 17:15)

Author's Note

A friend recently asked me why I would want to write a book like this and leave myself open and vulnerable. My answer was, "I can assure you with certainty it's not because I enjoy the feeling. This is what God has called me to."

I have tried to tell my story with as much transparency as possible in order that countless individuals may identify with the struggles I experienced throughout my healing journey. If you've ever been deeply wounded, if you've ever grieved the loss of a loved one, and if you struggle with a dependency, addiction, guilt, depression, fear, loneliness, anger, or bitterness, this book was written for you.

If you'll commit to doing the work of healing, meditate daily on the Scriptures in each section of this book, and walk with me through your own healing journey, God will meet you in a most amazing way. *He heals the brokenhearted and binds up their wounds* (Psalms 147:3).

I'll be praying for you.

—Grace Gayle

God Has a Plan for Your Life

"For I know the plans I have for you," declares the Lord,
"plans to prosper you and not to harm you,
plans to give you hope and a future."
(Jeremiah 29:11)

God's Purpose for Your Life

God created you to bring praise to Himself.
Bring my sons from afar and my daughters from the ends of the earth…
whom I created for my glory.
(Isaiah 43:6–7)

God's Purity

God's Holiness demands that we be holy.
Be holy, because I am holy.
(1 Peter 1:16)

The Problem is Our Sin

Sin: anything we think, do, or say that is not pleasing to God.
There is no one righteous, not even one; there is no one who
understands,
no one who seeks God.
(Romans 3:10–11)

For all have sinned and fall short of the glory of God.
(Romans 3:23)

The Punishment

God's righteousness demands that sin be punished.

For the wages [or penalty] of sin is death [eternity without God],
but the gift of God is eternal life
in Christ Jesus our Lord.
(Romans 6:23)

God's Provision

God's sinless Son took God's punishment for us.

Christ died for our sins according to the Scriptures,
that he was buried, that he was raised on the third day
according to the Scriptures.
(1 Corinthians 15:3–4)

For God so loved the world [insert your name] that he gave
his one and only Son, that whoever believes in him
shall not perish but have eternal life.
(John 3:16)

God demonstrates his own love for us in this:
While we were still sinners, Christ died for us.
(Romans 5:8)

God's Promise

Everyone is welcome.

Everyone who calls on the name of the Lord will be saved.
(Romans 10:13)

Whoever believes in the Son has eternal life, but whoever rejects
the Son will not see life, for God's wrath remains on him.
(John 3:36)

Your Participation

Believe and repent, acknowledge your sin to God,
and ask for His forgiveness.
Turn away from the way you used to live and purpose to live,
with God's help, a life that is pleasing to Him.
Believe in the Lord Jesus, and you will be saved.
(Acts 16:31)

If you confess with your mouth, "Jesus is Lord,"
and believe in your heart that God raised him from the dead,
you will be saved.
(Romans 10:9)

If we confess our sins, he is faithful and just and will forgive us our sins
and purify us from all unrighteousness.
(1 John 1:9)

Your Purpose

God created you to bring praise to Himself.
Thank Him for sending His Son to pay the penalty for your sin and
ask Him to help you live your life in a way that will be pleasing to Him.
In him we have... forgiveness of sins... in order that we... might be
for the praise of his glory.
(Ephesians 1:7, 12)

Your Commitment

I confess to God that I am a sinner and believe that the Lord Jesus
Christ died for my sins on the cross and was raised to life again on the
third day. I invite Him to come into my life and accept Him as my Lord
and Saviour.

Spiritual Healing

The Lord Is My Shepherd, by Elizabeth George
The Inward Journey, by Gene Edwards
Abba's Child, by Brennan Manning
The Search for Significance, by Robert McGee

Emotional Healing

Healing for Damaged Emotions, by David A. Seamands
A Door of Hope, by Jan Frank
Understanding Grief, by Dr. Alan D. Wolfelt
Boundaries, by Dr. Henry Cloud and Dr. John Townsend
Battlefield of the Mind, by Joyce Meyer

Sexual Healing

The Invisible Bond, by Barbara Wilson
Kiss Me Again, by Barbara Wilson

Healing Your Relationships

The DNA of Relationships, by Dr. Gary Smalley
The Freedom of Forgiveness, by Dr. David Augsburger
The Language of Love, by Dr. Gary Smalley and Dr. John Trent
Love's Unseen Enemy, by Dr. Les Parrott III

Healing Your Marriage Relationship

The DNA of Relationships for Couples, by Dr. Greg Smalley and Dr. Robert S. Paul

Love & Respect, by Dr. Emerson Eggerichs
The Power of a Praying Wife, by Stormie Omartian
The Power of a Praying Husband, by Stormie Omartian

Healing Relationships with Your Children

The Five Love Languages of Children, by Dr. Gary Chapman and Dr.
 Ross Campbell
The Blessing, by Gary Smalley and Dr. John Trent
The Key to Your Child's Heart, by Gary Smalley
The Power of a Praying Parent, by Stormie Omartian

Grace Gayle lives in Toronto, Ontario with her husband Paul and has three grown children. She works as a dental assistant and does freelance writing as a hobby. She also enjoys volunteering in long-term care facilities as a chapel speaker.